I0816266

Neither time nor dust can hinder your lust.

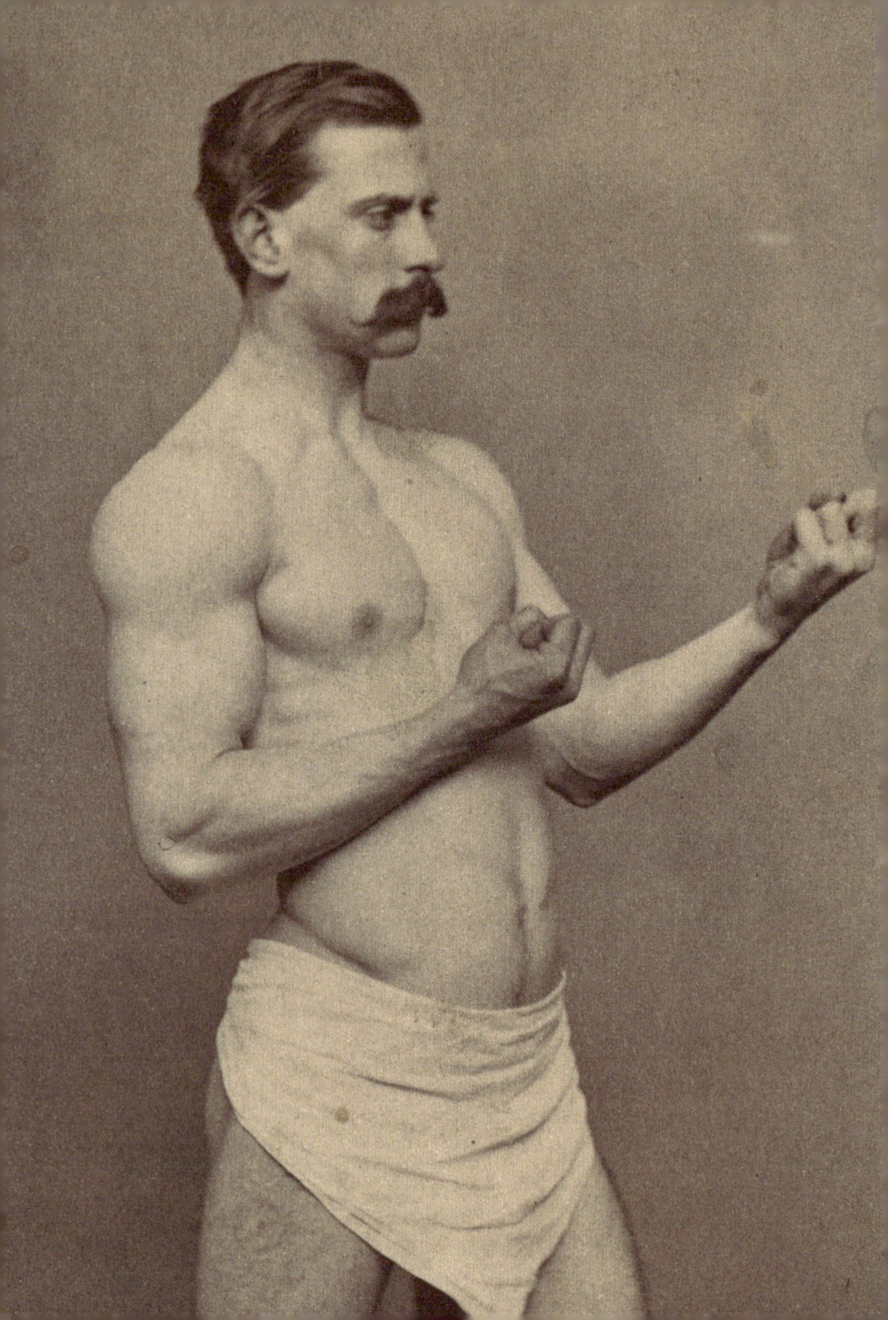

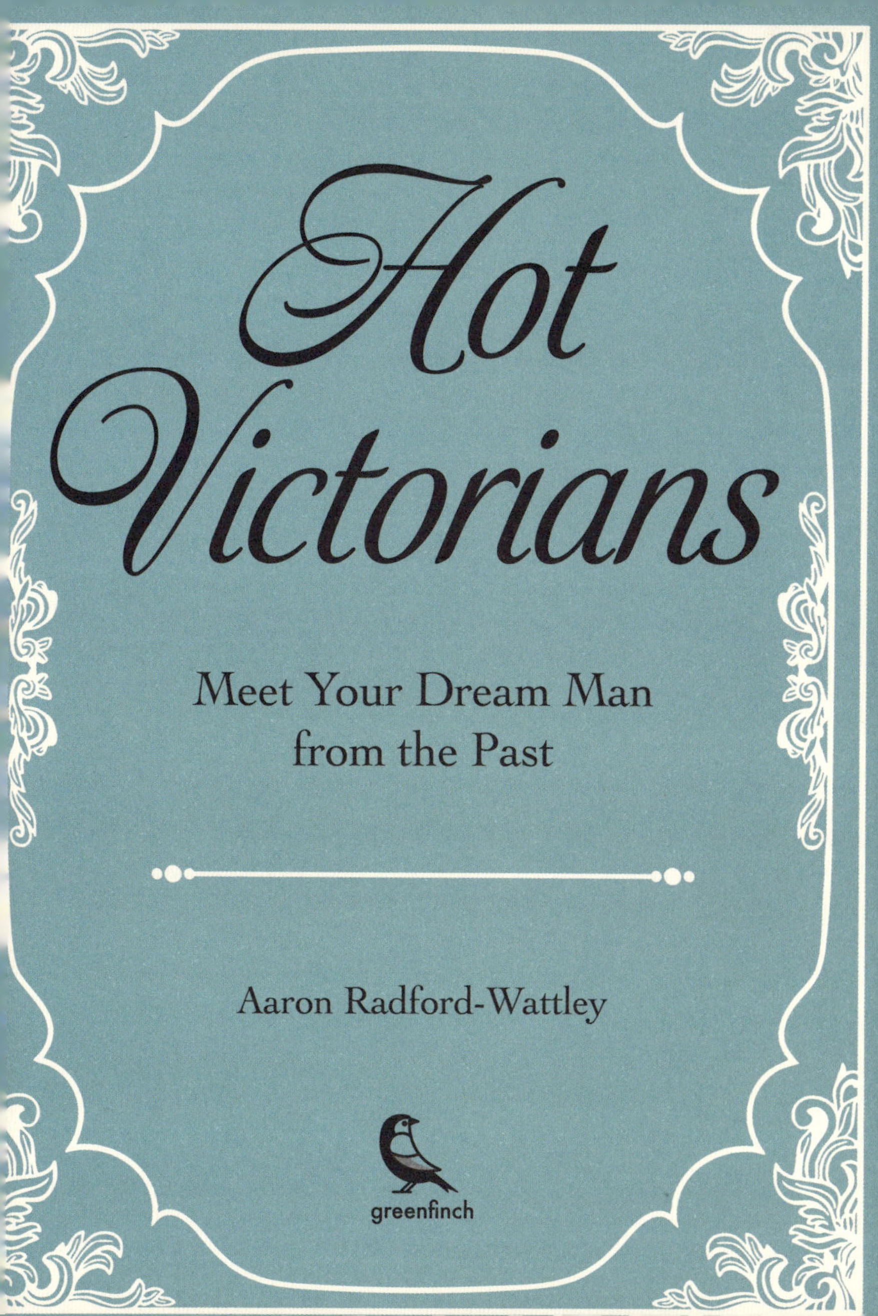

Hot Victorians

Meet Your Dream Man from the Past

Aaron Radford-Wattley

greenfinch

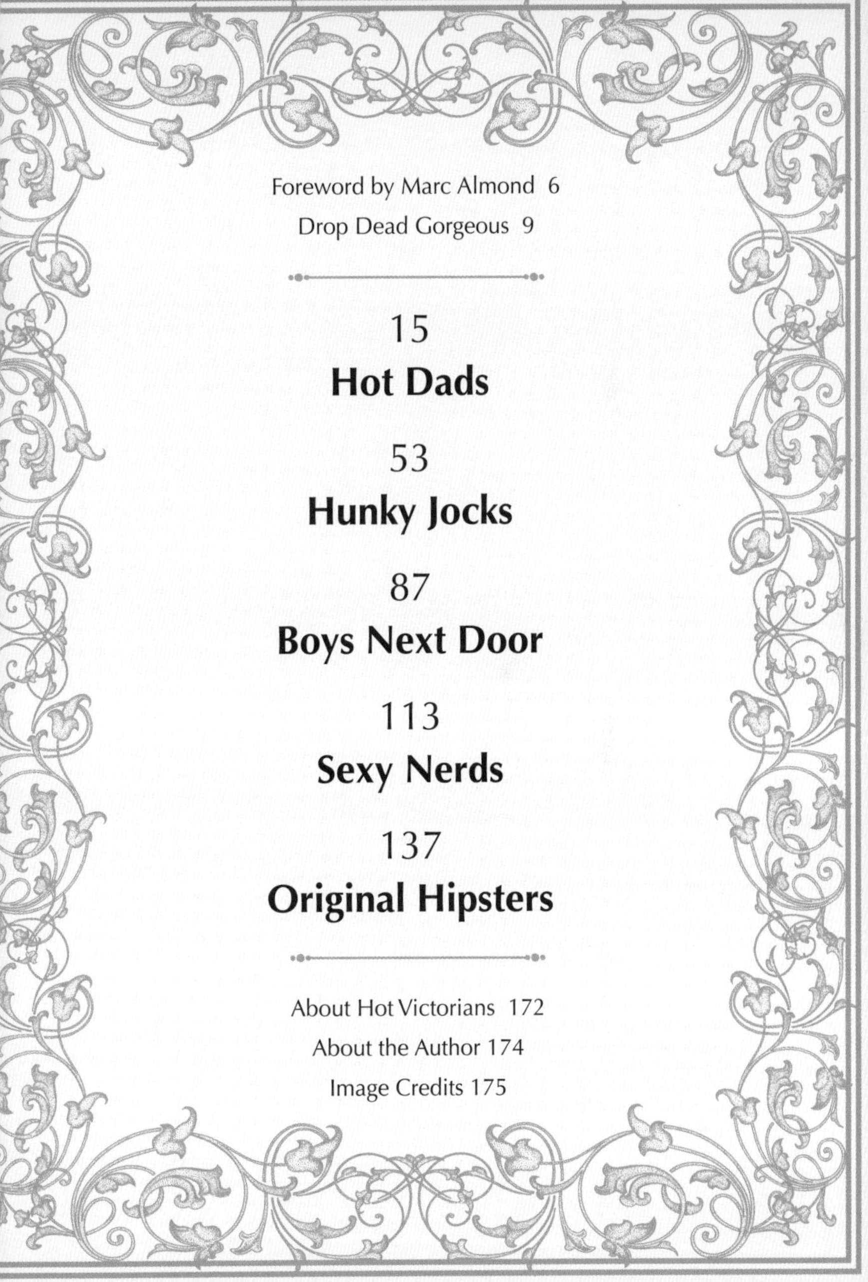

Yes, the Victorians were hot indeed

I am glad we have finally realised that the Victorians, particularly the Victorian Gentleman, were hot. Those stiff collars and buttoned-up suits were gifts waiting to be unwrapped. A loose shirt revealing a little skin, trousers just teasingly tight – not too much though, always the right side of respectable – and a stern poker face not giving anything away, hiding secrets that we can only guess at. With their moustaches and nicely trimmed beards, they were the very picture of well-groomed elegance. Victorians of colour and all nationalities and trades, the rough and the smooth alike. Yes, Victorians were hot indeed.

Marc Almond

(Soft Cell frontman and Hotness Connoisseur)

Drop Dead Gorgeous

There is something undeniably alluring about the men in photographs of the Victorian and Edwardian eras. You might have spotted some in a junk shop, at an antiques fair, or even online. With their often neutral expression, you may have wondered what they were like and who they were. On a few occasions, you might have even been startled at how attractive the sitter is, saying to yourself, "Damn, he's hot!" If you have ever experienced this, you're in for a right treat.

When you think of the time when these gentlemen lived, you naturally think of an age of rigid frigidity and decorum. A time when properness, decency and morality were all-important and all-encompassing. Of course, there is truth in this, but could unfathomable hotness still be found in such stifling social constraints? You bet your hobnailed boots it can!

The fashions alone are enough to make modern hearts flutter: immaculately tailored suits, high-collared shirts, and cravats tied in such a complex way that you'd think it were an algebraic equation. And let's not forget the facial hair – be it a distinguished moustache that furls elegantly at the tips or a full beard that looks as if it could whisper love sonnets aplenty, these chaps certainly knew the art of grooming.

And there is something to be said of the confidence often demonstrated in their poses. These chaps had a certain presence in their portraits – whether leaning casually against a chair, hand in pocket, or standing as proud as a peacock with a walking cane (purely for the rakish aesthetics, of course), they understood the importance of presentation.

Just look at those moody, sepia-toned shots of gentlemen staring intensely into the camera, eyes bright with latent passion. With the long exposure times of the age, it's understandable that these chaps look a little stern, unsmiling, and serious, but this surely only adds to their mysterious appeal. Maybe if you brush off the layers of dust, go behind the closed drapes, and peek through keyholes, you'll find that those living in the 19th and early 20th centuries were just as strong, sensual and hot as their modern-day counterparts.

Hot Victorians is a considered compendium of cuties for you to fall in love with. You're cordially invited to flip through the pages and enjoy the gentlemen of days long since passed. Each photograph, and every gentleman, tells a story of a life – of individuality, perhaps adversity, and always beauty.

By celebrating the allure of these long-gone chaps, *Hot Victorians* aims to highlight an often-forgotten truth: history isn't just about dates, events and notable figures – it's about people from all walks, their lives, and their stories. One very clear thing is that, whatever the decade, the century and the country, people have always been people, with the same hopes, desires, successes, flaws and allure.

So, give the maid a day off, sit back with a nice porcelain cup of tea, pull back the drapes and imagine what dating these magnificent men might have been like.

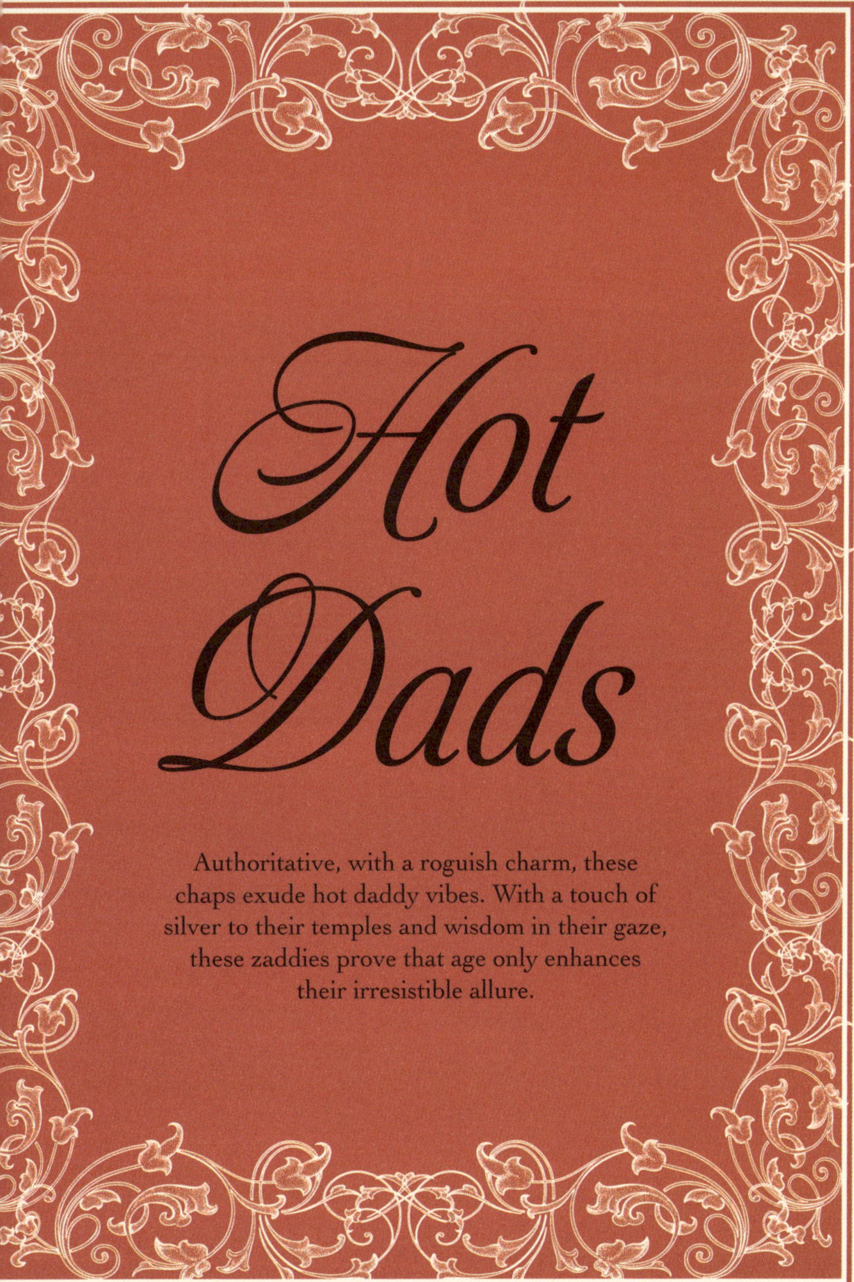

Hot Dads

Authoritative, with a roguish charm, these chaps exude hot daddy vibes. With a touch of silver to their temples and wisdom in their gaze, these zaddies prove that age only enhances their irresistible allure.

The Moody Military Man

Sir Peter Henry Scratchley (1835–1885)

Occupation: Military engineer and Special Commissioner for Great Britain, New Guinea

Born: Paris, France

Swipe if you like: Someone who looks perpetually peeved, but sexy with it

This Paris-born chap was the son of an English soldier. Taking career cues from dad, Scratchley attended the Royal Military Academy at Woolwich, and then began his career as an officer in the Royal Engineers. In 1859, after serving in the Crimean War, Scratchley was made Captain, and sailed off to the Australian colonies. While there, Scratchley successfully designed forts, including naming one after himself in Newcastle, New South Wales. He retired in 1882, gathering a raft of titles and roles, including Major-General, Special Commissioner for Great Britain, New Guinea.

My ideal Sunday includes...

A walk in the woods. And you can bet your boots that I'll insist on building us a fort whilst we're there.

My love language is...

Defence. A Netflix-and-chill session is likely to turn into a reconnaissance of your home where I'll identify all weak areas of security.

The Kalamazoo Cutie

Name unknown

Born: Michigan, US

Swipe if you like: Magnificent moustaches, music and celery

Hailing from Kalamazoo (yes, it's a real place), a city in the state of Michigan, this fine gentleman needs no cues for how to dress appropriately. With his pocket square fashioned into a three-point peak fold that echoes his wing tip collar, and well-manicured moustache, he is all about attention to detail.

Kalamazoo was once well known for its production of mandolins, cigars, paper, windmills and celery. So, it's not out of the realms of possibility that this young man worked in one of these industries.

I'll fall for you if...

You can make five non-boring dishes with celery as the main ingredient.

My idea of a perfect date is...

Most definitely a serenade of mandolins by moonlight. We'll both be dressed to impress and share a dish comprised of the Victorian answer to avocado – celery.

Bearded Naval Officer

Name unknown

Born: UK

Swipe if you like: Beards and cowlicks

Based in Mumbai, India (then called Bombay), this British naval officer had his portrait taken during the 1890s. After the opening of the Suez Canal in 1869, Mumbai became one of the Arabian Sea's largest and most important seaports, so our handsome, bearded gentleman would have been quite active. He may well have been involved in the Royal Indian Marine, which consisted of over fifty vessels engaging in a wide range of tasks, from surveying and carrying troops, to police and revenue duties.

One thing you should know about me…

When it comes to travel, I am most adventurous. But with food, much less so. I'm afraid I'm the kind of guy who will drag you to the ends of the Earth looking for a decent English breakfast, despite being on holiday. From Bombay to Barcelona, I demand a fry-up.

My biggest strength is…

My navigational skills. I will always be able to help you find where you parked your car; your drunkard, errant friend at a music festival; and the nightclub toilets. Together, we can chart the seas of love with ease.

The Cute Canadian

Mr Chrysler

Occupation: Unknown

Born: Ottawa, Ontario, Canada

Swipe if you like: High-society Canadians

This delightful image was taken in 1872 by William James Topley. Topley was an Ottawa-based photographer and businessman who rose to prominence in the early 1870s. He's noted for his portrait photography of the upper echelons of Canadian society, including prime ministers Sir John A MacDonald and William Lyon Mackenzie King. This photograph is of a man identified only as 'Mr Chrysler.' Whoever he was, he was certainly a handsome Ottawan.

Ask me about...

My intense passion for beavers. I am very pro beaver tail for wallets and beaver fur for hats. I'm a big beaver lover.

Boston Baby Blues

Name unknown

Born: Massachusetts, US

Swipe if you like: Big eyes, bow ties and Boston accents

This gentleman, with the most magnetic eyes, was photographed by A Marshall, a photographer based in Boston, Massachusetts in the 1860s and 1870s, when this cabinet card was created. An 1871 newspaper advertisement for the photography studio reads: 'A visit to Marshall's Rooms, 147 Tremont Street, and an examination of the specimens there exhibited, will show how tasteful and accurate is his work, and how attentive and painstaking he is to give entire satisfaction.' If only every date could be described as such. But this young Bostonian certainly is a fine specimen. Dressed to impress, he lures us in with his gentle, yet entrancing, eyes.

My ideal Sunday would be...

Walks along the cobblestone streets of Boston, debating Emerson versus Thoreau, followed by a few stouts in the Bell in Hand. And no, that's not a euphemism – it's actually one of the oldest bars in the US.

The Corn-fed Casanova

Name unknown

Born: US

Swipe if you like: Tumbles in the hay with Midwestern men who smell of sassafras

Hailing from Mason City, in the Midwestern state of Illinois, this gentleman had his photograph taken by S M Miller, sometime in the 1870s–1880s. With Mason City having only been established in 1857, this chap is likely to have come from elsewhere, a pioneer in search of exciting new opportunities.

This *carte de visite* captures the man's warmth, with his smiling eyes and perfectly groomed moustache. With a hint of a freckled complexion, this man was likely fair-haired, setting off his bright, light eyes, beautifully.

This gentleman is certainly the loving kind. As smooth as butter, he'd sweep you off your feet with one heck of a smile and a cheeky twitch of his 'tache. He'd be sure to defend your, somewhat shady, reputation at every town dance.

Dating me is like...

Churning butter – slow and steady, occasionally exhausting, strangely rewarding, but in the end, you'll have something rich, smooth and worth the effort. Let's discuss the price of corn over a sarsaparilla.

Love Shine a Light

Frédéric Auguste Bartholdi (1834–1904)

Occupation: Sculptor and painter

Born: Colmar, France

Swipe if you like: Big ideas and even bigger bow ties

If a suave, sophisticated artist is your thing, then look no further than Monsieur Bartholdi. Born in Colmar, France, this talented chap took drawing lessons as a youth, later studying sculpture and architecture in Paris. In 1869, Bartholdi pitched the idea of building a new lighthouse at the entrance of the Suez Canal. His design for the project was called 'Egypt Carrying the Light to Asia', and depicted a woman in neoclassical style wearing robes and carrying a torch up high. The design would not come to fruition due to the high costs of the project, but it wouldn't go to waste.

Two years later, Bartholdi suggested the idea of a large-scale statue as a gift from the French to the Americans in honour of the centennial of American independence. Much to his joy, his idea was approved. 'Liberty Enlightening the World' a.k.a. the Statue of Liberty, was officially unveiled on 28 October, 1886.

I'm looking for someone…

Who can hold a torch for me – figuratively and literally.

I'm overly competitive about…

Having the biggest erection. Eiffel? I've never heard of the chap.

Psychoanalysis and Chill

Sigmund Freud (1856–1939)

Occupation: Neurologist and psychoanalyst

Born: Moravia, Austrian Empire (now Czech Republic)

Swipe if you like: Lots of couch time and a sex obsession

Who could have guessed that young Freud was such a dashing daddy type? Known as 'the father of psychoanalysis', Freud was born into a Jewish family of wool merchants, yet pursued medicine instead of industry, becoming a clinical assistant to psychiatrist Theodor Meynert. In 1896, Freud coined the term 'psychoanalysis', a treatment that gained popularity among the social elite.

In 1938, with the Nazi occupation of Austria, Freud fled to London with the help of former patient Princess Marie Bonaparte and a written request to Berlin from US president, Franklin D Roosevelt. Freud settled in Hampstead, where his former home now houses the Freud Museum, London.

I'm looking for someone who...

Isn't afraid to explore the depths of the unconscious. Someone who won't mind a few 'slips of the tongue' and is willing to open up about their repressed desires.

Green flags I look for...

Are another's red flag – mother/father problems. I can be your daddy to help you work through those issues.

The Daydreamer

James Matthew Barrie (1860–1937)

Occupation: Author and playwright

Born: Kirriemuir, Angus, Scotland

Swipe if you like: A diminutive dreamer

Known as the creator of *Peter Pan*, Barrie was born and educated in Scotland, before settling in London, where he wrote successful plays and novels. In 1891, while casting a play, he met Mary Ansell, whom he later married. The Barries befriended Sylvia Llewelyn Davies and her five sons, who inspired *Peter Pan*.

The magical boy first appeared in Barrie's 1902 novel, *The Little White Bird*, followed by the 1904 West End play, *Peter Pan: The Boy Who Wouldn't Grow Up*. Eventually, the story became the famous novel depicting the adventures of Peter, a cheeky young boy who can fly and never grows up, a gang of Lost Boys, and a girl named Wendy, in the enchanting realm of Neverland.

I'm looking for…

My own Wendy Darling, darling.

My idea of a perfect date is…

A stroll through Kensington Gardens to visit my Peter Pan statue, but don't be put off if I occasionally get lost in Neverland (mentally, not geographically). I have the alarming habit of random clapping – after all, those fairies won't save themselves.

The Becoming Brooklynite

William George Alderton (1859–1919)

Occupation: Clothing salesman

Born: New York City, US

Swipe if you like: Dapper daddies

Good looks and classic British manners surely helped William make his way in late 1800s New York. Alderton was born to English immigrants; his father was a barber by trade, which clearly rubbed off on young William, with his perfectly coiffed hair. Alderton lived in Brooklyn in a (what is now) classic brownstone. The area was an exciting blend of cultures, with immigrants from across the globe, all living and working in the area. Alderton was a clothing salesman, no doubt making the most of his good looks, style and English etiquette to charm his customers.

You'll win me over if...

You always dress appropriately for the occasion. Be it a stroll in Prospect Park or a day out at Coney Island, 'Suitable attire at all times' is my motto. Oh, and if you know how to make a proper cup of tea, I'll fall at your feet.

Dating me is like...

Having your very own personal stylist who somehow knows everyone's inseam. Be prepared for unsolicited outfit advice and an innate ability to sniff out a sale from ten paces away.

Smooth Operator

Name unknown

Born: US

Swipe if you like: Manners, moustaches and lashings of Macassar oil

This dashing chap's likeness was captured in 1899/1900, a most elegant time for menswear, when peak Victorian style was striding confidently into the Edwardian era. And none could be quite so elegant or as confident as this gentleman. He was featured in a photographic album compiled by renowned sociologist and civil rights activist, W E B Du Bois. Naturally charming, this man looks as scholastic as he does dashing. He embodies an effective marriage of sophistication with approachability. With a gaze that is both confident and kind, he would smooth you over, like pouring (Macassar) oil on troubled waters, easing your fears and opening your heart with grace and ease.

Dating me is like...

A period drama. There will be a lot of rising tension, romantic build-ups and grand gestures. I believe love should be like a well-made candle – a slow burn.

Edinburgh's Finest

Name unknown

Born: Scotland, UK

Swipe if you like: A male Mona Lisa smile

In 1890s Edinburgh, we find this magnificent man, a part-time kilt model and full-time heartthrob. With wavy hair slicked into a beguiling rolling forelock and wearing a finely tailored suit, this hot Victorian could enchant even the most reserved of hearts. His smiling eyes are echoed in his lips that are threatening to burst out into a dazzling grin. At the time of this photo session, Edinburgh was a bustling city of Victorian Britain, with Princes Street and George Street, near where this photograph was taken, a hub of commerce. Clearly a man of the burgeoning middle class, he'd not have been short of a 'bawbee' or two, so the next wee dram in the local tavern would be on him.

If I were a drink...

I'd, of course, be a fine Scotch – smooth yet bold, and I get better with age.

You should date me if...

You appreciate the way I look in a kilt; easy access and I've got great calves.

The Ancient World Rocks Mine

Henry Peters Gray (1819–1897)

Occupation: Painter

Born: New York City, US

Swipe if you like: To be painted like one of his Greco-Roman girls

Good hair, immaculate dress sense and a somewhat vacant look that says either 'I'm contemplating the aesthetics of the ancient world' or 'Have I left the iron on?', dear Henry takes an intriguing photograph. Born in New York City, Gray entered the world of art first as a student at Hamilton College, Clinton, New York, and later as a student of the renowned artist Daniel Huntington. After studying works of the Old Masters in Florence and Rome, he returned to New York to forge a career as a professional painter. His time in Italy inspired many of his works, with influences echoing the Renaissance, apparent in his creations.

I go crazy for...

Anything to do with classical antiquity. The clean lines of Roman columns, the alabaster statues and the gods of ancient Greece, all set my heart ablaze.

My idea of a perfect date would be...

You and me in my studio. You're draped in a makeshift toga holding a vase aloft, and I with my easel at the ready.

The Modernizer

Alfred Stieglitz (1864–1946)

Occupation: Photographer, art dealer and promoter

Born: Hoboken, New Jersey, US

Swipe if you like: Avant-garde art, a no-nonsense attitude and an impressive soup strainer

A champion of the arts is always a most attractive character trait in a man. And none were quite as dedicated and attractive as Mr Alfred Stieglitz. Alfred was educated in Germany before returning to the US with a newfound passion for photography. His father supported his ambitions, even buying Alfred a photography business.

Stieglitz's influence was monumental: he became vice-president of the Camera Club of New York, and took over *Camera Notes*, the world's first photography magazine. Alfred also went on to found 291, an iconic art gallery on New York's Fifth Avenue. The gallery showcased avant-garde works, including those of Georgia O'Keeffe, his muse and future wife. Few have combined passion and artistry like Stieglitz, and he realized his mission, cementing photography as a true art form.

My ideal weekend includes…

Convincing everyone I meet that photography is a bona fide art form, arguing about modernism over coffee, and taking moody photographs of clouds that absolutely symbolize my feelings. Bonus points if you're Georgia O'Keeffe.

Father Time

Name unknown

Born: Waltham, Massachusetts, US

Swipe if you like: A man so reliable you can set your watch by him

This gentleman is a true daddy in every sense of the word. On the back of the photo (taken by photographer William Alexander Webster in Waltham, Massachusetts, *c.* 1880s) is written, 'My father'. Well, whoever wrote those words, they were lucky to have such a good-looking man as their father. His kind eyes and adorable cleft chin surely made many hearts flutter. We can only assume that his hometown was Waltham, known as 'Watch City' ever since the American Watch Company first opened its doors in 1854. It's quite possible that this dashing daddy was involved in the timepiece trade – he looks the reliable, dependable type, always on time and considerate with yours.

My best chat-up line is...

Is that a watch in your pocket or are you just happy to see me?

The Bold, Brave and Bearded Brightonian

Edward Carpenter (1844–1929)

Occupation: Writer, poet, philosopher and activist

Born: Brighton, UK

Swipe if you like: Progressive vegetarian men

Daddy lovers will certainly appreciate the silver-foxy and forthright Edward Carpenter. Although not a household name today, his importance can't be overlooked. Carpenter was an early advocate for gay and women's rights, challenging Victorian social norms with his intelligence, charm and radicalism. He was also a strong advocate for prison reform, vegetarianism, recycling and nudism.

Carpenter was acquainted with some of the most influential people of his time, including Oscar Wilde, E M Forster, Walt Whitman and Isadora Duncan. His scientific book published in 1908, *The Intermediate Sex: A Study of Some Transitional Types of Men and Women*, bravely explored the complex nature of gender and sexuality. His belief that love between men should be celebrated, rather than suppressed, laid the groundwork for many LGBTQIA+ rights movements.

Truth or dare?...

Truth: I think we should make a return to nature, live in communes, eat a plant-based diet and challenge outdated notions of love and gender. Dare: I dare you to read some of Walt Whitman's poetry with me ... naked.

On the Nose

Name unknown

Born: Plymouth, UK

Swipe if you like: A nose so Roman, it has its own empire

Undeniably handsome, this gentleman's *carte de visite* was taken in Plymouth during the 1870s by John Hawke. You can't help but notice the sitter's prominent nose, and it's likely that Hawke couldn't either. Hawke, and the gentleman in question, have chosen to showcase the strong feature to great effect, with a side-profile shot. The photograph has an altogether regal and stoic nature, with a strength that echoes the statues of ancient Rome.

My controversial opinion is that...

My nose is not a flaw, but a beautiful character trait that makes me uniquely me. It majestically leads the way, much like a figurehead on a mighty ship. And like that figure, I do hope you'll hold on to me for dear life.

The Fit, Fiery Farmer

Marion Butler (1863–1938)

Occupation: Politician, lawyer and farmer

Born: Sampson County, North Carolina, US

Swipe if you like: Bearded agrarian daddies

A tempestuous man from rural North Carolina, Marion Butler was a Populist leader, and a force to be reckoned with. With a surprising flair for bucking traditions, Marion was born on a farm but became a high-flying politician. Perhaps these humble beginnings were fertile soil for someone who would later champion the working class. Butler had a love of learning and graduated with a degree in law from the University of North Carolina. He took over the family farm on his return, later becoming the leader of the Farmers' Alliance, going on to win election to the North Carolina Senate as a member of the Democratic Party. Known for his impassioned speeches and tireless advocacy, Butler served in the US Senate from 1895 to 1901. Later in life he returned to practising law and farming.

My simple pleasures...

I love the smell of manure in the morning. I also enjoy the confusion my first name causes the family and friends of my date.

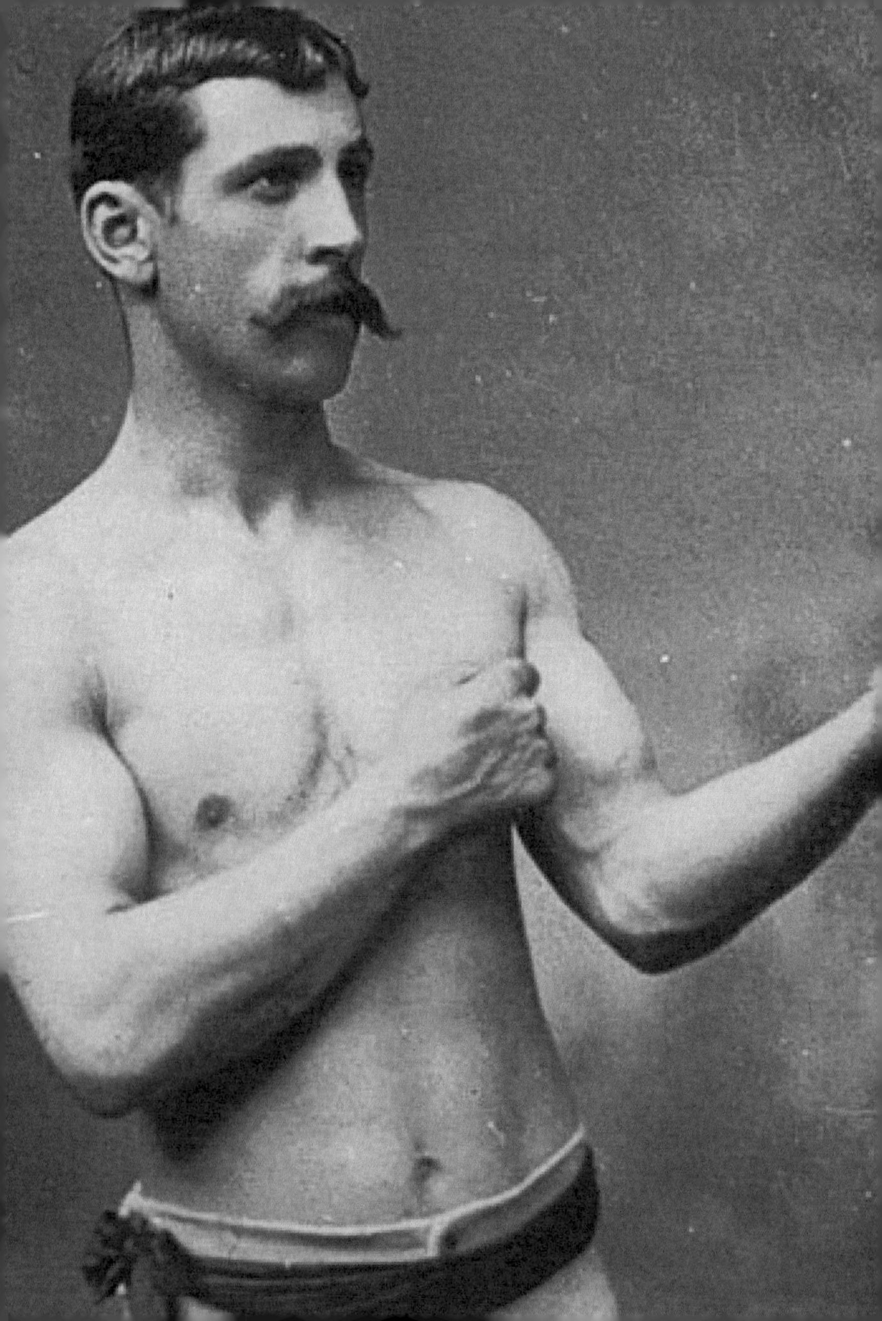

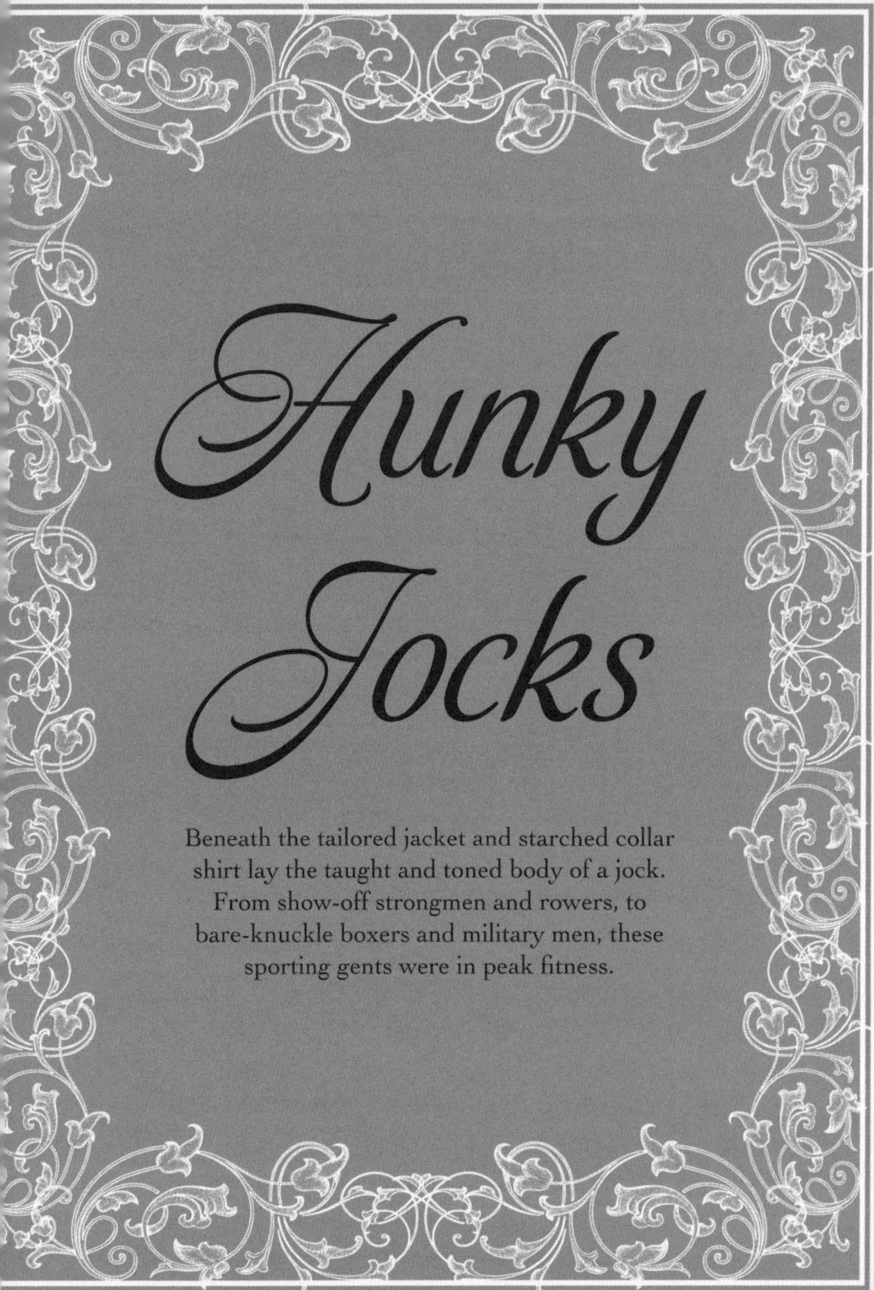

Hunky Jocks

Beneath the tailored jacket and starched collar shirt lay the taught and toned body of a jock. From show-off strongmen and rowers, to bare-knuckle boxers and military men, these sporting gents were in peak fitness.

The Show-Off Strongman

Eugen Sandow (1865–1925)

Occupation: Bodybuilder and showman

Born: Königsberg, Prussia (now Kaliningrad, Russia)

Swipe if you like: Muscles and lots of them

A fanatic of health and fitness, Sandow was an early pioneer of keeping in shape, earning him the title 'the father of modern bodybuilding'. This Prussian-born German gained international attention after winning a competition in London in 1889. This victory led Sandow to make appearances across Britain, his bulging muscles delighting audiences up and down the country. He is pretty much the archetypal Victorian strongman, complete with a statement moustache and a fig leaf for modesty.

My secret phobia is...

I have a very real fear of leaf blowers. Glue only goes so far.

I'm not keen on...

Clothes. When your body is as hot as mine, it's rather selfish to cover oneself, don't you agree?

Master Stroke

Edward 'Ned' Hanlan (1855–1908)

Occupation: Professional oarsman, hotelier and alderman

Born: Toronto, Canada

Swipe if you like: Riparian romps

Mr Hanlan is often thought of as Canada's first sporting celebrity. Growing up on the Toronto Islands, Hanlan would row from Hanlan's Point (named after his father John and the family hotel) across the harbour to school in Toronto – a distance of some 5 km (3 miles). His passion and natural ability for rowing led him to become an amateur champion of the Toronto Bay. Around the age of 20, Hanlan started his professional rowing career, and by 1884 he was the world sculling champion, a title he held for five years in a row.

Ask me about...

The nudist beach I share my name with. Meet me there?

My greatest strength...

I always find a way to stick my oar in.

The Bodacious Boxer

Peter Jackson (1861–1901)

Occupation: Heavyweight boxer

Born: Christiansted, US Virgin Islands

Swipe if you like: Someone who is tough, yet dandy, in a fight

Born in the Virgin Islands, Jackson was an Australian boxer of international fame. He was someone who could knock you out with one punch or disarm you with his dazzling dress sense. After building a sterling career in Australia, Jackson fought his way across America, the UK and Ireland. Jackson won 57 out of his 105 fights, with 29 wins by knockout, and I don't mean by his looks.

I geek out on...

Top hats. I have a vast collection and seize every opportunity to don one. When it comes to dating me, I'm a brim-full.

Pretty as a Pitcher

Michael 'Mickey' Welch (1859–1941)

Occupation: Major League Baseball player

Born: Brooklyn, New York, US

Swipe if you like: Unrivalled ball skills and beer

Nicknamed 'Smiling Mickey', this cheerful baseball legend is surely one you'd love to get your mitts on. Born in Brooklyn to Irish immigrant parents, Welch went on to play for several professional baseball teams. He is most famous for his three Major League seasons with the Troy Trojans, and 13 with the New York Gothams (later known as the Giants). Welch would go on to hold the record for the most consecutive batters struck out (nine) on 28 August, 1884. This record would not be broken until 1970. Welch was inducted into the Baseball Hall of Fame in 1973.

I'm looking for…

Someone who can handle my curveballs.

My personal motto is…

'Pure elixir of malt and hops, beats all the drugs and all the drops.'

Over-Under Lover

Gilbert Laird Jessop (1874–1955)

Occupation: Cricketer

Born: Cheltenham, UK

Swipe if you like: Squat men in cricket whites with grass stains

This quintessentially English cricketing gentleman debuted for his county cricket team at 20 years of age. Jessop was not a large man, standing at just 5ft 7in (170cm), and his stature and stance when playing earned him the nickname 'The Croucher'. Despite his stocky build, he was a fielder of fantastic speed and is thought to have been the fastest run-scorer in cricket history.

Together we could...

Avoid the sticky wickets of life.

I go weak at the knees over...

The sound of willow on leather.

You'll bowl me over if...

You attend all my matches and know how to remove grass stains.

Bicontinental Biceps

Charles 'Charlie' L. Norton (1852–1889)

Occupation: Boxer

Born: Birmingham, UK

Swipe if you like: Prime cut English beef seasoned with a side of moustache

Poise, posture and prowess are essential in boxing, and this pretty pugilist had them all. One of the unsung greats of boxing, Norton won his first professional fight in 1869, which was bare-knuckled and lasted two hours and 10 minutes. He went on to win the Lightweight Championship in 38 rounds at St Helena Gardens near Birmingham in 1878. Word of Norton's skills led him to become a boxing instructor at the Birmingham Athletic Club. The following year, Norton upped sticks across the pond to the US, settling in Newark, New Jersey. In 1881, Norton won the Lightweight Championship of America by default as his opponent had declined the invitation to fight.

This year I'd like to be…

Yours, if only by default.

You should not date me if…

You insist on touching my moustache. You may have free rein on my biceps as compensation.

A Man in Uniform

Walter Daniel Tull (1888–1918)

Occupation: Professional footballer

Born: Folkestone, UK

Swipe if you like: Premier League top totty

When it comes to excelling on both the football pitch and the battlefield, this Kentish cutie is your man. Born by the seaside to an English mother and Barbadian carpenter, Walter Tull discovered his football skills early in life. He worked a printer apprenticeship, but he kept his eyes on the ball, and came to the attention of Clapton FC. He stayed with the team until 1909, when he was signed by Tottenham Hotspur. He would go on to play for other top teams, including Northampton Town and Glasgow's Rangers. During World War I, he served in the Middlesex Regiment and was commissioned as a second lieutenant.

My greatest loves are…

Football and my country. Could you be my third?

Can You Handle(bar) This?

Léon Hourlier (1885–1915)

Occupation: Cyclist and pilot

Born: Reims, France

Swipe if you like: Handlebars. Both the moustache and the ones found on bicycles.

Toned, taut and undeniably tasty, Frenchman Léon Hourlier was a professional cyclist. He won the French national cycling championships in 1909, 1911 and again in 1914, when he also won the Grand Prix de Paris. During World War I both he and his brother-in-law Léon Comès (who was also a cyclist) enlisted in the French Air Force as volunteer pilots. Tragically, they died together in a plane crash on 16 October, 1915.

I geek out on...

Le vélo, of course. I'm so keen on spreading my knowledge and passion for bicycles that, in 1913, I published a cycle training manual for young cyclists, called, *The Bike, How I Train, Advice for the Young, etc!* Are you willing to go the distance with me?

My idea of a perfect date would be...

On a bicycle built for two, of course!

6433

The Svelte Seine Swimmer

Albert Bougouin (1886–1960)

Occupation: Swimmer and mechanic

Born: Paris, France

Swipe if you like: A handyman who looks great in a one-piece

Bougouin, while not the tallest of men, was like a coiled spring in the water, torpedoing his way to victory. He came to international attention as a swimmer in 1905, after taking part in the first Traversée de Paris à la nage, a 7 mile (11.6km) race in the Seine. He dropped out mid-race but tried again in 1906, when he placed first, making it in three hours, six minutes. Later that year he also won the swim across Toulouse. During World War I Bougouin served as a cyclist and utilized his skills as a mechanic, leading him to be seconded as a special officer with a mechanical engineering firm. Later in life he opened a bazaar in Pantin, Paris.

A daily essential...

I like to get a few strokes of every kind in before breakfast.

I won't shut up about...

The importance of a reinforced gusset. I've lost several bathing suits as they simply don't hold up to vigorous wear.

Manners Maketh This Man

Charles Wreford-Brown (1866–1951)

Occupation: Cricketer and footballer

Born: Clifton, Bristol, UK

Swipe if you like: Deep pockets and sportsmanship

Charles was truly a player, in every sense of the word. Good looks, charm and expert sporting skills made him a star of Victorian football and cricket. Born into an affluent family, Wreford-Brown attended Charterhouse School, going on to study at Oriel College, Oxford. While at Oxford, he played cricket and football for the university. By the 1890s he was playing for Corinthian Football Club, an amateur club that had an ethos of fair play and sportsmanship. While captaining the England football team, Wreford-Brown once came on to the pitch with his deep shorts pockets filled with gold sovereigns that he promptly handed to each player after scoring a goal.

My greatest strengths are…

Ball skills aside, my manners. I could charm the knickers off a nun.

Green flags I look for…

Good etiquette and generosity. Of money, time and oils. Much of my outgoings are on linseed for my bats, lotions for my balls, and oils for my hair and 'tache.

The East End Bruiser

Hezekiah Moscow a.k.a. Ching Ghook (c. 1862–1892)

Occupation: Boxer, music hall entertainer and lion and bear tamer

Born: The West Indies

Swipe if you like: Exceptional pectoral muscles

Who knew that jodhpurs and a sash could be so alluring? Clearly, Hezekiah Moscow did. Born in the West Indies and living in London's then gritty East End, Moscow was a boxer who also moonlighted as a music hall entertainer, sparring on stage. His boxing career began after an alleged bar-room brawl instigated by racism in a Spitalfields pub in 1882. In 1888, Moscow took part in exhibition boxing at the Sebright Music Hall. When he wasn't showing off his mean left hook, he worked at the East London Aquarium as a lion and bear tamer.

The best piece of advice I was ever given...

Don't poke the bears in the zoo. They pack a punch better than I do.

I'm looking for someone who...

Knows how to apply baby oil. Liberally and lovingly, please.

My greatest strength is...

I can last many, many rounds. In the ring, in the pub, everywhere.

The French Sailor

Name unknown

Born: France

Swipe if you like: Gallic goatees

Toulon, where this sexy seaman was stationed, is a beautiful city on the French Riviera. It's also the main base for the French Navy. This sailor took time out of his busy schedule to pose for a cabinet card, resplendent in his naval regalia. With model-level good looks and a Breton-striped shirt, you'd be forgiven for mistaking this for a Jean Paul Gaultier fragrance ad campaign from the 1990s, but this photograph is actually from about a hundred years earlier, *c*. 1880–1890s.

My love language is...

Writing love letters, *ma petite sirène*. They may be so florid that even Suzette (Toulon's most popular lady of the night) would blush, but the existential poetry of my writing will win you over. After all, everyone loves a sailor.

Private Parts

Private Nash

Born: Massachusetts, US

Swipe if you like: Men who always rise to the occasion

Who doesn't love a man in uniform? This is an immediately eye-catching chap, confidence shining as bright as his buttons surely were. Identified only as 'Private Nash', this photograph was taken in 1885 at Amherst, Massachusetts, so he was possibly a student at the Massachusetts Agricultural and Military College. Founded in 1863, the MAMC (today, The University of Massachusetts Amherst) was a well-known institution, offering courses in engineering, agriculture, horticulture and mathematics, as well as a strong cavalry programme.

Military service was mandatory for students, and our Private Nash would have performed everything from bayonet and sabre exercises, to guard-mount and outpost duty. In inclement weather, Nash would have broken a sweat in the Drill Hall. We can only daydream whether we would have been classmates.

I'm the kind of guy...

Who can plough a field at dawn, perform a perfect close-order drill at noon, and still have enough gusto for a fervent tumble in the stables.

Ask me about...

My salute – it's impressive and isn't the only thing that stands at full attention when required.

Let Me Be Your Teddy Bare

Theodore Roosevelt Jr (1858–1919)

Occupation: Politician and 26th President of the US

Born: Manhattan, New York City, US

Swipe if you like: A rugged outdoorsman with a soft spot for animals

This strapping chap is none other than Theodore 'Teddy' Roosevelt Jr. You'd be forgiven for thinking this was a stereotypical Brit abroad, in days gone by, when the wearing of a knotted hanky and the rolling up of trousers was the beachwear *du jour*. But no, this is the 26th President of the United States in his salad days. Roosevelt is seen here (partly) wearing sculling gear while an undergraduate at Harvard, in about 1877.

As President, Roosevelt was known for his booming voice and toothy smile, as well as being a strong advocate for progressive reforms and conservation. His passion for nature made a lasting impact: in 1902, during a hunting trip in Mississippi, Roosevelt refused to shoot a tied-up bear, deeming it unsporting. The story made headlines, inspiring the creation of the 'teddy bear'.

Hanging out with me...

Is an all-American outdoors adventure. One minute we'll be having a deep discussion about the importance of conservation, and the next I'll be taking you mountain-climbing. My bear hugs are legendary.

GL. FLOTTAN.

Nauti-cal but Nice

Carl Emil Pettersson (1875–1937)

Occupation: Sailor, explorer and King of Tabar

Born: Stockholm, Sweden

Swipe if you like: A Scandinavian Robinson Crusoe

This Swedish dish of a man began his seafaring life when he was about 17. The sailing life took him to lands far-and-wide, but it was a trip in the Pacific Ocean that most made a mark on Pettersson's life. On Christmas Day, 1904, the ship he was sailing on, the SS *Herzog Johann Albrecht*, sank off the coast of the New Ireland Province. He survived and found himself washed up on a beach on Tabar Island. He was discovered by locals who brought him to their king, Lamy. Lamy's daughter Princess Singdo, so struck with this Scandinavian sailor, fell in love with Pettersson, and the two were married in 1907. After the death of the king, he took on the role of monarch. He and his wife had nine children.

My superpowers are...

I can make a happy home wherever I roam. Tom Hanks in *Cast Away* has nothing on me. Could you be my Wilson?

The Overly Confident Colonel

Colonel William Edward Van Wyck (1841–1915)

Occupation: Paper merchant and Colonel

Born: New York, US

Swipe if you like: Taut torsos, 'taches and tiny towels

Some chaps are so proud of their physique that they insist on showcasing their buffness at every opportunity. Colonel Van Wyck was no different. A native New Yorker, he was a paper merchant and partner at C F Hubbs & Co. Photographed by Jeremiah Gurney & Son in 1866, Van Wyck would have just got back from fighting in the Civil War.

After active service, William returned to his main profession in the paper trade, but kept up his fitness in the New York Athletic Club, later serving as its president. With confidence in spades and not a hint of shame, Van Wyck would not bat an eye if he was caught after taking a morning shower on the landing in his altogether, be it by your mother or housemate. He would just grin, stroke down his impressive 'tache and strut like cock-of-the-walk into your bedroom. The witness would be helpless to resist admiring his pert derrière as he goes past.

My best feature is…

Well, it's hard to pick just the one, so I'll narrow it to three: my hefty biceps, my magnanimous moustache and my bottom. It's rather impressive, so firm that you could bounce a penny off it.

Boys Next Door

Approachable and dependable, these young lads were the type mothers (and hopefully you) would love. Expect charming smiles, tousled hair and a happy-go-lucky outlook, all while having that rare handsome-but-doesn't-know-it-yet quality.

The Dishy Doctor

Dr Arthur Leslie Shidler (1860–1899)

Occupation: Doctor

Born: Indiana, US

Swipe if you like: George Clooney in his *ER* era crossed with Henry Cavill

Arthur grew up on his parents' farm before moving to Chicago, where he graduated from the College of Physicians and Surgeons in 1886. Dr Shidler started practising medicine in earnest in Ellisville, Illinois, specializing in problems of the eye, ear, nose and throat.

I geek out on...

Anything to do with ENT. I'm a passionate otolaryngologist, so swollen throats, blocked ears and perpetual nose bleeds really stoke my fire. I may be waxing lyrical about ear infections, nasal polyps or sleep apnoea, but as I stare into your eyes, looking for signs of conjunctivitis, you'll be utterly lost in mine.

Hold Your Horses

Bert Martin (c. 1879)

Occupation: Farmhand and horse thief

Born: Missouri, USA

Swipe if you like: An 'expert borrower of steeds'

Bright-eyed with an infectious affability, little is known about Bert's early years. As a young adult, he moved around Nebraska and worked on a farm, where his good looks caught the eye of Lena Dean, the farmer's daughter. The two were married in haste in 1899 in a classic 19th-century American shotgun wedding. Bert, wanting to support his family, fell on the wrong side of the law and took to 'borrowing' animals. In 1900, Bert was tried and convicted of horse theft. Almost a year into his sentence, Bert's cellmate hinted to prison guards that they might want to take a closer look at Bert. The prison doctor declared that Bert was biologically a woman (we might now use the term 'intersex'). The intriguing story hit papers across Nebraska, and in early 1902, Bert's sentence was commuted to 18 months, on the proviso that he not re-offend and he was immediately released.

I'm looking for...

Someone to rein me in. I'm no stranger to horseplay, I like to do things on the spur of the moment, and sometimes I stirrup trouble. Ultimately, I'm looking for my better hoof.

3656

Want to be Teacher's Pet?

Pinkney Thompson Miller (1859–1947)

Occupation: Principal

Born: Winchester, Tennessee, US

Swipe if you like: A high-achieving teacher

Drive, determination and dedication are always attractive and usually pay off. Case in point – Pinkney Miller Sr. Born in Tennessee, Miller's father was a carpenter, while his mother was busy looking after several children. Pinkney worked hard to better himself and his prospects and became a schoolteacher in Evansville, Indiana. Pinkney worked his way up to Assistant Principal, and later Principal.

Dating me is like…

Being in a classroom. There is lots of room for learning, you're graded on your performance, and playtime is always your favourite part of the day.

Golden Boy

Gustav Klimt (1862–1918)

Occupation: Artist

Born: Vienna, Austria

Swipe if you like: Someone who thinks outside the box, and gilds it

This raffish young man embodies the 19th-century Central European artist, with his dishevelled hair, beard and somewhat come-to-bed eyes. After studying art in Vienna, Klimt, his brother and a friend worked together on art commissions. These works helped Klimt establish a career as a painter of murals and ceilings. But it was Klimt's works after 1897 that established his unique brand of symbolism and eroticism, focusing on women. Klimt's ostentatiously bold use of gold leaf in his most famous artworks, *The Kiss* (1907–1908) and *Portrait of Adele Bloch-Bauer I* (1907) became part of what is known as his 'Golden Phase'.

My one controversial opinion is…

Gilding the lily is no bad thing. Gilding a beautiful woman is even better – I like to think that I inspired Ian Fleming's *Goldfinger*.

Dating me is like…

Stepping into one of my paintings. Deliciously chaotic, beautifully detailed and just a bit overwhelming. I'm likely to show up on a date with flecks of gold leaf in my beard.

Babe Behind Bars

Frank Curran (1872–?)

Occupation: Gasfitter

Born: Ireland

Swipe if you like: A crooked, tattooed Cillian Murphy

He may have been something of a bad lad, but when your mugshot looks as hot as this, who cares? Born in Ireland and later emigrating to the US, Curran lived in the Upper East Side of Manhattan, New York City, and worked as a gasfitter. At a little over 5 ft 8 in (1.72 m) tall, he didn't have great stature, but with his black hair and grey eyes, he was a handsome chap. Work as a gasfitter clearly didn't pay much, as Curran was arrested on 9 April, 1894, trying to improve his income with burglary. On his arrest card, he is noted as having quite a few intriguing tattoos: an anchor with a star in the centre, the letters F.C. on the inside of his right forearm, and a crucifix on the inside of his left arm.

My secret superpower is…

Breaking and entering…into your heart.

Dating me is like…

Dating a jewel thief/cat burglar. Your heart is a vault that I can slip into without a key.

Jaw-dropping James

James Wilkerson

Occupation: Unknown

Born: Kansas, US

Swipe if you like: A strong jawline and a strong boutonnière game

While we only have his name and image, you can see the natural elegance and handsomeness of James Wilkerson. He'd definitely be someone you could confidently bring home to mother, and one that you'd have to hide from your single friends. James was a local from Leavenworth, Kansas. In 1892, Wilkerson sat for a local photographer who liked to hone their craft of portraits. The impressive collection of images dating from the 1860s–1930s included many portraits of African Americans, which are now an important historical record held by the Amon Carter Museum of American Art in Fort Worth, Texas.

My greatest strength...

Is my natural charm. Mums love me. Some a little too much. You have been warned.

Bashful in Bayswater

Name unknown

Born: UK

Swipe if you like: Shy, curly-haired guys

This fine young man, whose name is sadly lost to time, certainly came from a family of means as the photographer was based in London's affluent Bayswater during the 1880s and 90s. The sitter could have been a student at one of Britain's top universities perhaps, or an apprentice at a family firm. Starting a new chapter of adulthood, he maybe wanted to mark the occasion with a distinguished photograph, capturing his luscious locks, showcasing his burgeoning sideburns, all whilst giving a somewhat coquettish Princess Diana glance.

All I ask is that you...

Don't touch my hair. It takes a lot of time and product to look this good.

Ask me about...

My gentleman's take on the Curly Girl Method. Chaps can use it too, and to great effect (please see my photograph for evidence).

A Young Hopeful

Name unknown

Born: Adrian, Michigan, US

Swipe if you like: Naivety and clearly defined boundaries

Handsome in his first flush of youth, this young man's likeness was captured in this cabinet card sometime between the late 1880s and 1891. Photographer Mr Julius A Foster had 'photographic parlours' in the centre of Adrian, where this chap sat for his portrait.

Adrian, home of our bachelor, was known as 'the wire fence capital of the world', after John Wallace Page established the successful Page Woven Fence Company around 1884. By 1895 the company would be the largest employer in Adrian. Perhaps this gentleman was an employee of the company? Maybe an apprentice office clerk?

I'm looking for someone...

To bring down the fences I've put up around my heart. I have clearly defined boundaries, which I guess have been hardwired into me since I was a boy. But, like a badly made wire fence, I'll snag you in a jiffy.

A date with me would include...

A short trip on the new electric street railway service, then a stop at the soda fountain to share a phosphate soda. Maybe a cheeky peck on the cheek behind the fence factory? But nothing to get the town's rumour mill churning, of course.

Dashing Daguerreotype Dandy

Name unknown

Occupation: Unknown

Born: US

Swipe if you like: Rosy cheeks and Wolverine-esque hair

Taken circa 1855 in Rochester, New York, this daguerreotype captures one very handsome young man. He looks as if he might have some very strong opinions on the importance of a well-formed cravat. Tied once or twice? He would surely know the answer. And with that romantically waved hair, he is exuding mid-19th-century chic.

Ask me about…

The importance of a cane. Such a simple accessory truly makes one's outfit.

This year I really want to…

Grow mutton chops. I think they would frame my face well and set off my windswept locks.

Yorkshire's Finest

Name unknown

Occupation: Unknown

Born: Yorkshire, UK

Swipe if you like: A guy your mum and gran will love

A bit of a mystery man, we do know that this photo was taken in 1891 or 1892, and that the sitter comes from 'God's Own County', Yorkshire. He's certainly the kind of guy that's handsome but doesn't know it. His latest attempt at growing a moustache has made him the butt of his boisterous friends' jokes, but he always just laughs and flashes his devastatingly charming smile, and all negative banter disappears.

I won't shut up about...

The correct way to make a cup of tea. You can probably guess my preferred brand.

I'll fall for you if...

You can make perfect gravy without any lumps. The same goes for custard. I love lashings of both.

Dating me is like...

Wearing your favourite pair of boots: reliable, broken-in but built to last.

Brasenose College Man

Name unknown

Occupation: Student

Born: UK

Swipe if you like: Posh collegiate totty. A Victorian version of *Brideshead Revisited*

This fine chap is from a photo album that once belonged to playwright George Louis Pleydell Bancroft (1868–1956). Bancroft attended Brasenose College in the late 1880s, where this gentleman was a fellow student. Brasenose was founded in 1509 and is one of the constituent colleges of the University of Oxford. The gentleman in this photograph appears to be a member of the college's Octagon Club, a wining and dining social group. He looks every bit the gentleman but after a few scotches too many, anything could happen.

Unusual skills…

I can easily sink 12 ports and sing *God Save the Queen* whilst standing on my head without so much as a raised eyebrow.

My love language is…

Compliments on my grooming and attire. Especially my patent slippers and my strong socks game.

The Light-fingered Lothario

Görtz Birger Adolfsson Hinderfors (1885–1941)

Occupation: Pipe worker

Born: Jönköping, Sweden

Swipe if you like: Tall men with even taller rap sheets

Some gentlemen really can make a mugshot work to their advantage, and Herr Hinderfors is no exception. Taken in Stockholm in 1908, this mugshot captures an understandably stern Hinderfors after his arrest for theft. This wasn't his first time in front of the Stockholm police's camera, and it wouldn't be his last, as he was arrested again for theft in 1913. So, consider keeping your eye on your valuables and taking your bag with you when you go to the restroom on a date with Görtz.

Crime aside, Görtz has some most attractive particulars: He's described as tall, blond, blue-eyed and with facial scars. If you just think of him as slightly shop-soiled merchandise, you could have a very happy relationship.

The way to win me over is...

To hide your heart somewhere I can't steal it. Though, to be honest, I'll probably try.

My idea of a bad first date...

Would be a visit to a jewellery shop. I'm not very good with temptation. The only drawers my fingers should be in are yours.

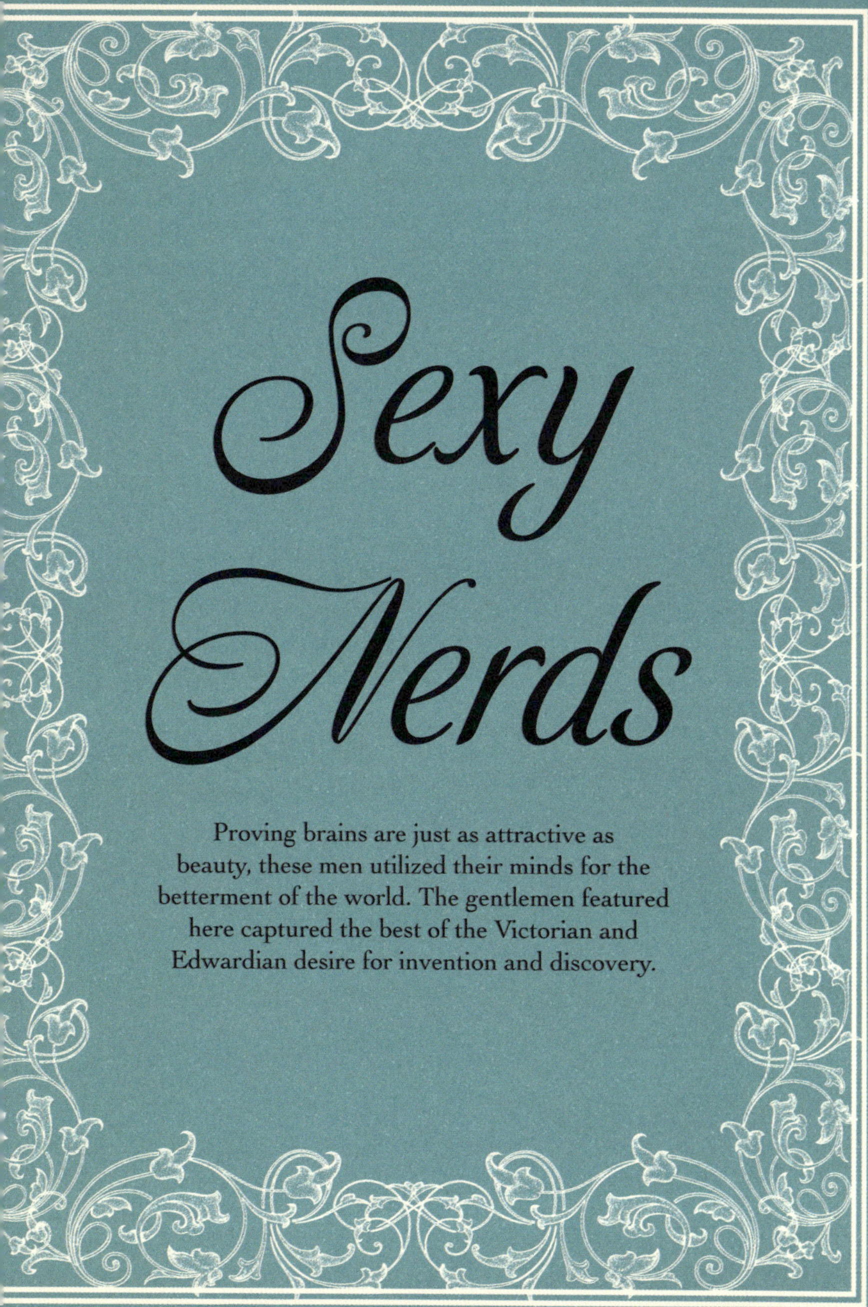

Sexy Nerds

Proving brains are just as attractive as beauty, these men utilized their minds for the betterment of the world. The gentlemen featured here captured the best of the Victorian and Edwardian desire for invention and discovery.

The Sexy Scientist

Alexandre Yersin (1863–1943)

Occupation: Physician and bacteriologist

Born: Aubonne, Switzerland

Swipe if you like: Brains more than brawn. Think Brian Cox meets Luke Wilson

Quite remarkably, Yersin identified the bacillus responsible for the bubonic plague, which was later named in his honour. Yersin also showed that the same bacillus was present in the rodent – as well as in the human strain of the disease – thereby highlighting the likelihood that rats were a source for transmission.

Green flags I look for...

Someone who doesn't see mouldy bread as something to throw away, but a potential source of new discoveries.

I most fear...

Rats! Sometimes they look cute, but I have a sneaking suspicion they may be one of the world's most deadly creatures.

The Pretty Polymath

Edward Heron-Allen (1861–1943)

Occupation: Polymath, writer, lawyer, violinist and Persian scholar

Born: London, UK

Swipe if you like: A pretty boy who's a bit of a know-it-all but makes beautiful music. Literally.

Mr Heron-Allen was a true Renaissance man with a passion for a wide range of subjects including science, languages and zoology, with particular enthusiasm for Persian literature and the violin. Heron-Allen's love of the violin developed further into learning how to craft the instruments himself. He even published several books on the matter.

Dating me is like…

Dating a beautifully bound encyclopaedia, with gilded edges and about ten volumes. I pretty much know everything and will be your go-to 'phone-a-friend' on game shows and a regular in the local pub quiz.

I geek out on…

Why, violins of course. I can wax lyrical about the pros and cons of a Stradivarius and I admire the form of a well-constructed violin the way most chaps appreciate a beautiful woman.

Chemistry a Must

Name unknown

Occupation: Chemist

Born: Sweden

Swipe if you like: A lover man in a lab coat

Taken at the turn of the 20th century, this young man was captured in his laboratory, most likely in Uppsala, Sweden. This suave scientist sits rather nonchalantly on his stool, test tube in hand, hoping to be on the very cusp of an important scientific discovery that will change humanity forever…or at least remove armpit stains from white shirts.

I'm looking for…

Straight-up chemistry, a chain reaction. Someone to ignite the flames of my heart, burning brighter than a Bunsen burner at full throttle.

My love language is…

Someone who rinses out their beakers and always makes sure the gas stove is switched off.

Harvard Grass is Always Greener

Richard Theodore Greener (1844–1922)

Occupation: Professor and diplomat

Born: Philadelphia, Pennsylvania, US

Swipe if you like: A man who comes first

Richard was the kind of man who made history just by walking into a room. This incredibly handsome man had it all – good looks, academic excellence and an inspiring fortitude of character. Having an early thirst for education, with a background that consisted of a mix of homeschooling, self-taught and formal school, Greener went to Harvard College, where he earned a bachelor's degree, making him its first Black graduate. He added to this success with a law degree at the University of South Carolina, where he would later become its first Black professor. His expertise in law, philosophy and elocution set him in good stead for his appointment in 1898 as America's first Black diplomat to a white country (Russia).

Green flags I look for...

If you're something of a sesquipedalian with perfect pronunciation. I love those who are orally gifted.

Ask me about...

My elocution skills. I've won the Bowdoin Prize at Harvard, twice!

A Selfie-Made Man

Robert Cornelius (1809–1893)

Occupation: Photographer and manufacturer

Born: Philadelphia, Pennsylvania, US

Swipe if you like: A little light play

Born to a Dutch immigrant silversmith, who worked as a chandelier manufacturer, Cornelius was surrounded by the magic of light from an early age. After studying chemistry, he worked with his father, where he came into contact with photographers, who he supplied with the plates required for the first widely available photographic process – the daguerreotype. Cornelius became interested in the medium, experimenting with photography, including handcrafting a camera obscura.

In 1839, a self-portrait Cornelius took in the yard behind the family's store, became the first selfie taken in recorded history. Due to the long exposure time required in daguerreotype, Cornelius is estimated to have had to hold his pose for up to 15 minutes.

My superpower is...

I can look devastatingly dashing with whimsical, windswept wonder, whilst in actuality, I'm standing perfectly still.

I'm looking for someone...

To be still with. If you can hold my attention for up to 15 minutes, you'll capture both my heart and a decent dag'.

A Son of a Preacher Man

Sir Henry Solomon Wellcome (1853–1936)

Occupation: Pharmaceutical entrepreneur

Born: Almond, Wisconsin, US

Swipe if you like: An inquisitive man with enquiring eyes

Mr Wellcome had a pretty dour upbringing, with his father a missionary and enthusiastic temperance man. Young Wellcome found solace in his passion for medicine, graduating from the Philadelphia College of Pharmacy & Science in 1874. Together with his friend Silas Mainville Burroughs, Henry founded the pharmaceutical company Burroughs, Wellcome & Co., which is credited with introducing tablet medicines to England.

Wellcome's lifelong fascination for all things medically related saw him amass a huge collection of artefacts. After his death in 1936, much of this collection was distributed to other collectors and museums, and today you can see a fascinating, and sometimes, macabre selection, in London's The Wellcome Collection.

My simple pleasures are...

Hunting high and low for historical medical items. You best-believe I'm the kind of chap to riffle through your bathroom cabinet in the morning after the night before.

Ask me about...

My most prized possession – Napoleon's toothbrush. Made of silver gilt, bone, and horsehair, 'tis quite the thing to behold.

The Inci-dentally Dishy Dentist

Name unknown

Occupation: Dentist

Born: US

Swipe if you like: Snazzy waistcoats, smouldering eyes, and free dental care

Taken in the mid 1800s, this daguerreotype shows a young dentist plying his trade proudly. You could forgive him for what he may do to the back of your less-than-perfect molars because he is just so thoroughly handsome. With an intense gaze that's saying either, 'Are you free for dinner?' or 'Is that a misaligned jaw or do my eyes deceive me?', you're certainly intrigued by his intentions. Despite the rather threatening way he wields his pliers, the dapper waistcoat and dandy necktie go some way to easing your nerves.

I'm looking for…

Someone to fill in the gaps of life. I want to crown that special someone as my one-and-only love.

The Bookish Babe

James Brown (1800–1855)

Occupation: Publisher

Born: Acton, Massachusetts, US

Swipe if you like: Books and the men who publish them

Brown entered the world of work as a servant to the family of Levi Hedge. Hedge was a professor at Harvard, Massachusetts, who introduced Brown to the classics and mathematics, broadening both his intellectual and professional horizons. Brown later took work as a shop boy for publisher William Hilliard, later becoming a clerk at his publishing firm, Hilliard, Gray & Co. After the company dissolved, Brown joined Charles C Little & Co, becoming a partner in 1837. The firm was renamed Little, Brown and Company in 1847.

Brown specialized in publishing law books and British poets, as well as importing foreign editions. He is celebrated in book form in a biography, *A Life of Mr Brown*, by George S Hillard, published in 1855.

Spending time with me...

Is very much like reading a good book. At first, you'll pass me off as just a nice volume with fancy gilded edges, but with every turn of the page, you will discover new depths, hidden footnotes, and every date will be a plot twist that will make sticking around worth your while.

The First Cut is the Deepest

Sir Hamilton Ashley Ballance (1867–1936)

Occupation: Surgeon and military man

Born: Clapton, Middlesex, UK

Swipe if you like: A steady-handed lover

Born into a privileged and successful family, Ballance was the fourth son to enter the medical profession, following his brother, surgeon Sir Charles Ballance. After studying science at King's College, London, Hamilton trained at University College Hospital, including as house surgeon, house physician and senior obstetric assistant. Later, Ballance became assistant surgeon at the Norfolk and Norwich Hospital. With the outbreak of World War I, Ballance rose from Major to temporary Colonel, serving as a consulting surgeon for armies in France. After the end of the 'Great War', Balance became a Knight Commander of the Military Division of the Most Excellent Order of the British Empire (KBE).

Ask me about...

The best method of approach in severe cases of appendicitis. I'm a veritable samurai with a scalpel.

My superpower is...

My strong constitution. I've seen things that would make a butcher nauseous, so there's no need to be embarrassed about that hair clogging up the bathroom plughole.

The Debonair Doctor

Dr Arthur Melvin Townsend Sr (1875–1959)

Occupation: Doctor and pastor

Born: Winchester, Tennessee, US

Swipe if you like: A debonair man of many callings

As the son of a Reverend, it's no surprise that Townsend would follow in his father's footsteps, and become a pastor. But Townsend was not just passionate about matters of the soul; he was also very interested in matters of the body. He attended and graduated from Roger Williams University (an historically Black college in Nashville, Tennessee) in 1898, and graduated with honours from Meharry Medical College in 1902. Townsend applied his brainpower to the research of pellagra, a disease caused by lack of niacin. Alongside his medical work, Townsend played the organ for several churches, and led Sunday school classes in hospitals and jails, giving hope and healing to those in need.

Dating me is like…

Attending a Sunday service – my chat game can sometimes come across as a sermon but you'll hear some divine music and will always come away feeling uplifted.

My perfect date would be…

Going to church followed by a slap-up Sunday lunch of niacin-rich foods.

The Aerodynamic Aristocrat

Armand Antoine Agénor de Gramont, 12th Duke of Gramont (1879–1962)

Occupation: Scientist and nobleman

Born: Paris, France

Swipe if you like: A man who's aroused by the lift-to-drag ratio

Gramont was the wealthy grandson of a duke and a baron, but was not one to fritter his days away in decadent hedonism. Gramont followed his interests in science, particularly in aerodynamics. So dedicated to his passion was he, that in 1908 Gramont founded a laboratory in the grounds of a retirement home in Levallois-Perret.

In 1911, he wrote a thesis entitled, *Essai d'aérodynamique du plan'(Aerodynamic Test of the Plane)*, the first of its kind in France. Gramont then won the Fourneyron Prize, from the French Academy of Sciences, along with fellow aerodynamics enthusiast Gustave Eiffel (who designed the Eiffel Tower).

I'm looking for...

Someone to go through the wind tunnel of life with. We may experience some turbulence, but together we can navigate our way to a love that truly soars.

One of my bad habits...

I tend to fold every piece of paper I find into a plane.

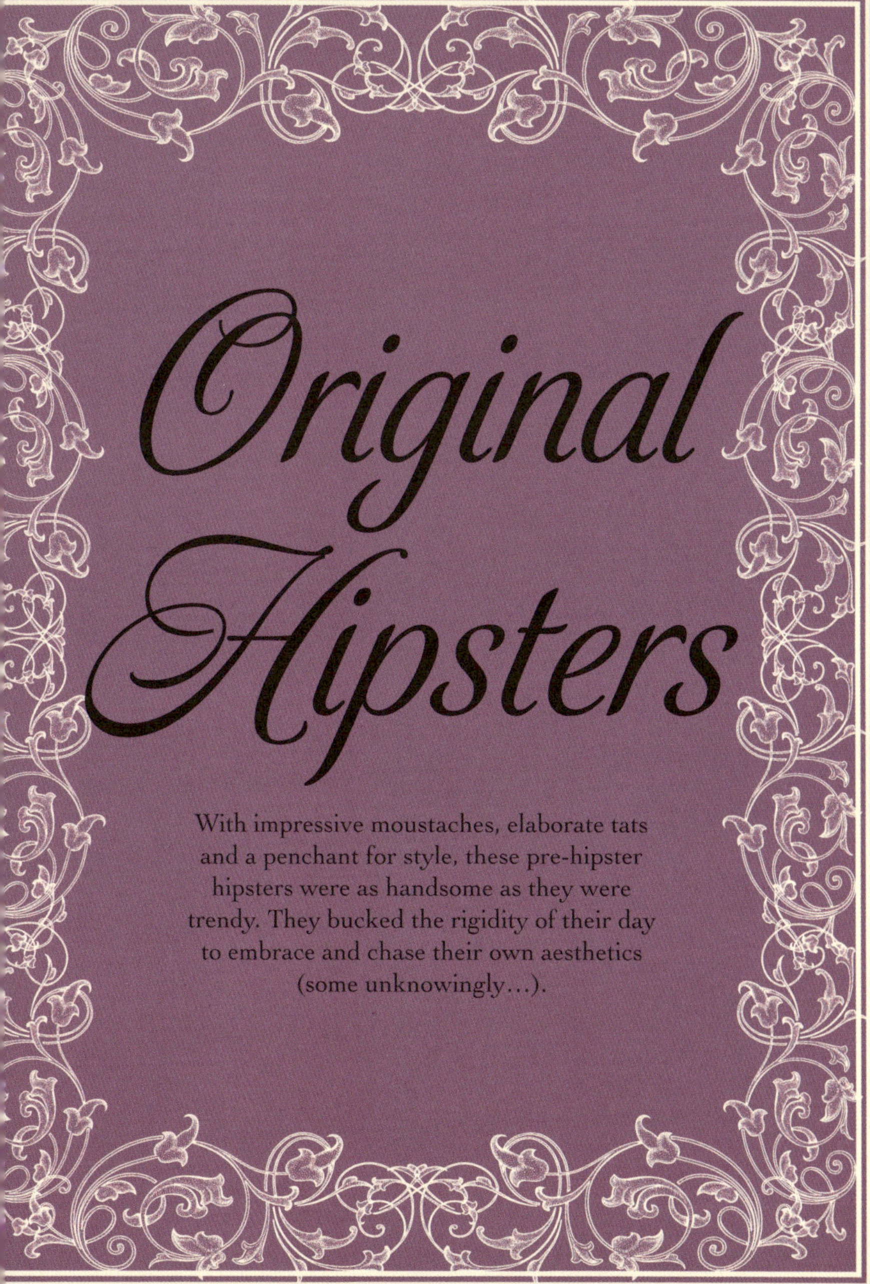

Original Hipsters

With impressive moustaches, elaborate tats and a penchant for style, these pre-hipster hipsters were as handsome as they were trendy. They bucked the rigidity of their day to embrace and chase their own aesthetics (some unknowingly…).

The Bejewelled Maharaja

Sir Sardar Singh Bahadur GCSI (1880–1911)

Occupation: Maharaja of Jodhpur State

Born: Jodhpur, Rajasthan, India

Swipe if you like: A man with expensive tastes

Dashing and decadent, Sir Sardar Singh Bahadur GCSI, was the Maharaja of Jodhpur State from 11 October 1895 until his death on 20 March 1911. He succeeded his father, Maharaja Sir Jaswant Singh II in 1895. Soon after becoming a Maharaja, he began to spend state funds at an alarming rate and pursued pleasures instead of his duties – a true hedonist. His frivolous spending soon depleted state revenues, but check out the results. Looking this good costs money.

I spend most of 'my' money on...

Silk robes, jewellery and polo horses. You'll likely be paying for dinner.

Dating me is like...

Using your overdraft on a night out – a good idea at the time, but in the long run, not very sustainable.

The Damn Fine Dentist

Oda Nobuyoshi (1860–1926)

Occupation: Physician, bacteriologist and dentist

Born: Sukumo, Japan

Swipe if you like: Great teeth and hipster model vibes

Who said dentists can't be hot? A case in point is Nobuyoshi, a dentist who pivoted his medical career to dentistry in mid-1880s Japan. This move paid off with Nobuyoshi going on to open his very own dental practice in 1886, relocating to Hakusai Hospital (Obiyamachi, Kochi City). By 1925, the building of Nobuyoshi's Oda Dental Clinic in Masugata, Kochi City, was completed and is still operational today.

Something that's non-negotiable for me is...

Good oral hygiene. Obviously. Ask me to demonstrate the correct way to brush your teeth. I consider this foreplay.

The Tortured Artist

Rafael Romero de Torres (1865–1898)

Occupation: Painter

Born: Córdoba, Spain

Swipe if you like: Bearded Iberians

Do you desire a classic brooding artist, paired with dark and handsome looks? Then Señor Rafael Romero de Torres is your man. Coming from a family of artists, with his father and two brothers all accomplished painters, he joined the profession too. He won several awards for his art, but an event in 1890 knocked his creative confidence. The National Exhibition of Fine Arts, Spain, originally awarded Romero de Torres a second-class medal, a placing he was rather pleased with. But after some reconsideration by the judges, the second-class medal was retracted and given to another entrant. Instead, he was awarded a third-class medal. It's been said Romero de Torres never fully recovered from this.

I'm looking for...

Someone to be the light that I can never truly possess.

You'll win me over by...

Showering me with praise. Tell me I'm a better artist than my brothers and father and that awards don't matter, and I'm yours.

Dashing Dallas Dandy

Isham Woolridge (*c.* 1870–1915)

Occupation: Barber

Born: Arkansas or Mississippi, US

Swipe if you like: An immaculate, well-groomed man

Step into a world of romance, wit, pomade and the occasional unsolicited opinions on your haircut with this barber from Dallas. With strong bow tie game, this dapper chap is Mr Isham Woolridge. Born in either Arkansas or Mississippi (records differ), this elegant man lived in a house he owned (quite an accomplishment) in the Deep Ellum neighbourhood of Dallas. Deep Ellum had been a thriving hub for African-American culture since the 1870s.

My love language is...

Making other people feel good about themselves through grooming. That, and a decent-sized tin of moustache wax.

You'll come for...

My good looks and charm, and stay for the free consultations.

The Customized Cowboy

Name unknown

Occupation: Cowboy

Born: US

Swipe if you like: Furry chaps (the trousers, not men)

During the peak of what is known as 'The Wild West', it's estimated that around a third of cowboys were African American, something many Western films have ignored. With skills including horse-riding, rounding up cattle, roping and branding, to name but a few, it was a hard, but essential, calling. I doubt most ranch hands were as well turned out as this gentleman. With a waistcoat decorated with appliqué motifs and pom-pom trims, he had an eye for style and a strong personality.

You'll lasso my heart…

If you can tie a Honda knot in under 50 seconds.

The one thing to know about me is…

Yes, the hat comes off, but the boots stay on.

The Smouldering Smith

Name unknown

Occupation: Blacksmith

Born: Likely Philadelphia, US

Swipe if you like: Moody metalworkers

With a glowering gaze like hot coals, this burly and surly blacksmith could (s)melt hearts and morals with one mighty blow of his hammer. He doesn't see his occupation as just a job, it's an art form. If you're looking for someone to hammer out your commitment issues, this is your guy. His rolled-up shirt sleeves show he's not shy of a hard day's work and he's ready to forge something lasting with someone that truly stokes his fires.

My unusual skills…

I can talk to horses. They don't talk back as of yet, but still…

A deal-breaker for me is…

Someone who has too many irons in the fire. You only need one. Me!

The Noetic Navajo

So Hache

Occupation: Navajo warrior

Born: Navajo Nation, US

Swipe if you like: Extremely photogenic guys

So Hache, a young Navajo Native American warrior, is pictured here circa 1907 in a photograph by Carl Moon. With his model-quality bone structure and stoic expression, the camera loves him just as much as anyone with eyes. So Hache is the kind of man who is quiet with his words but very demonstrative of his passions through deeds and actions. He doesn't talk things through endlessly, instead, he contemplates deeply and acts with a swift strike akin to that of a startled snake. Honestly, who needs a cowboy when you have this guy?

My secret superpower is...

I can find the perfect light any time of the day.

We'll get along if...

You appreciate 1990s new-age music. It gave me a second life.

Criminally Hot

Carl Wiktor Blom (1873–1938)

Occupation: Sheet metal worker

Born: Häggesled, Sweden

Swipe if you like: Naughty Nordic men

A metalworker by trade, Carl lived and worked in Stockholm. In October 1896, this Swedish dish was arrested for crimes unknown (but likely theft and/or fraud). Standing at just 5 ft 6 in (1.6 m) he's not your typically tall Scandinavian man but he sure could take a mugshot. Think of him like that shabby house at the end of the street – many would advise against buying it, but with a little TLC (and a bit of reform) you could end up with something special.

The best way to ask me out is by…

Checking with my probation officer. The law might not be on my side, but time is certainly is.

The Vivacious Vicomte

Armand Georges Odet de Montault (1827–1913)

Occupation: Nobleman and *bon vivant*

Born: Paris, France

Swipe if you like: Bachelors, dandies and drinkers of brandy

The Vicomte (equivalent to a British viscount) Odet de Montault was renowned in French society and this image truly captures his sophistication, elegance and *savoir faire*. The way he glances at us hints at an element of mystery, with just a dash of 'come hither'. Armand's pose exudes a slight 'devil-may-care' attitude, topped off perfectly by the cigar held louchely in the corner of his noble mouth.

Your place or…?

Definitely mine. I live in the Château de Baclair, in Nointot, Normandy. If your pile of bricks is larger, we may come to some suitable arrangement.

I won't shut up about…

The importance of a fine cigar and a superior brandy to round off a meal.

A second date with me includes…

A spot of falconry on my estate. I think it makes for the perfect bonding activity.

Love Through a Lens

Franz Benque (1841–1921)

Occupation: Photographer

Born: Ludwigslust, Germany

Swipe if you like: Trachten jackets, beards and long exposure times

This thoroughly pre-hipster hipster was a German photographer who saw the profession as a wonderful new way to express himself, especially through portraits. Benque's career began with lessons from photographer C C Hersen in Güstrow, a town in north-eastern Germany. Benque moved to Trieste (then part of the Austro-Hungarian Empire) at the beginning of 1864, in response to an advertisement that Guglielmo Sebastianutti, a watchmaker and goldsmith at the time, had published in a German newspaper with the aim of finding a business partner. The meeting resulted in the founding of a successful photographic studio that they ran together for almost 20 years.

My best chat-up line is…

Are you a camera? Because every time I look at you, I develop feelings.

A Wonder from Down Under

Rupert Charles Wulsten Bunny (1864–1947)

Occupation: Painter

Born: Melbourne, Australia

Swipe if you like: Men who like mythology

This utterly striking gentleman's smile is beyond infectious. Mr Bunny was born and raised in Melbourne, Australia, to a well-to-do family. His father was a court judge, and his family's wealth afforded young Rupert to take long trips to Europe, leaving him adept in both French and German.

Bunny's first entry into the world of art was at Melbourne's National Gallery School of Design. Wanting to build upon his burgeoning skills, Bunny moved to London to study, followed by Paris, where La Belle Époque was in full swing. During this time, his artistic style veered from mythology to pre-Raphaelitism. Bunny enjoyed a most cosmopolitan life during his years in Paris, socializing with such talented contemporaries as Auguste Rodin and Claude Debussy, and receiving a bronze medal at the 1900 Paris Exposition Universelle.

The first round (of absinthe) is on me if...

You know Greek mythology. Call me your Dionysus from Down Under.

My love language is...

Dropping the occasional French word or expression into a sentence. I want an instant *coup de foudre*.

The Bohemian Bachelor

William Michael Rossetti (1829–1919)

Occupation: Writer

Born: London, UK

Swipe if you like: Artistic musings and foppish fashions

Mr Rossetti was an English writer born to the exiled Italian Gabriele Rossetti and Frances Polidori. His siblings included Christina (a writer), Dante Gabriel (a poet and artist) and Maria Francesca (an author and nun). With such a family it's no surprise that William, too, would have a strong artistic and creative flair.

Most famously, Rossetti was one of the founders of the Pre-Raphaelite Brotherhood. The group, created in 1848, was a somewhat-secret society of writers, artists and critics that included Rossetti's brother Dante Gabriel, William Holman Hunt, John Everett Millais, Frederic George Stephens and Thomas Woolner.

You should go out with me to save me from…

My epic monologues on Pre-Raphaelite art.

Dating me is like…

Joining the Pre-Raphaelite Brotherhood. There will be endless poetry recitals, heated debates on art, and occasional awkward moments when I compare you to one of Botticelli's maidens.

The Magnetic Man on a Mission

George Edward Anderson (1860–1928)

Occupation: Photographer

Born: Salt Lake City, Utah, US

Swipe if you like: Twinkling eyes

If you're looking for true commitment, then Mr Anderson is your chap. He's a dedicated follower of the Latter-Day Saints, and an avid photographer, so you'll be lucky to be his third passion. Specializing in portraiture and documentary photographs, Anderson entered the world of photography as a young apprentice to Charles Roscoe Savage. Aged just 17, Anderson, along with two brothers, established their own photography studio. The business was a success, allowing Anderson to open studios in Manti, Springville and Nephi, Utah. Anderson was called to serve a mission to England in 1907. On his return he resumed his photography with a studio in South Royalton, Vermont.

Dating me is like...

Processing a photograph. It takes time, patience and the right chemistry.

I'm the kind of guy who...

Will make you feel like the centre of the universe, mostly because I'll spend several minutes taking your photograph.

The Ink-credible Guy

Hori Chiyo (1859–1900) or his apprentice, Horisei

Occupation: Tattoo artist

Born: Japan

Swipe if you like: Beautifully intricate tattoos and the men who create them

For those with a love of an inked guy, this handsome man from Japan is just the ticket. Taken by photographer Suzuki Shin'ichi II, sometime during the Meiji period (1868–1912), this tattooed man is thought to be tattooist Hori Chiyo. However, some scholars believe it could be Hori Chiyo's apprentice, Horisei, showing off his master's handiwork.

The reopening of Japan to the Western world in 1853 afforded outsiders the opportunity to get Japanese tattoos. Foreign sailors were among the first in the queue, but later, in 1881, perhaps unexpectedly, Prince Albert Victor and Prince George of England also got tattooed by Hori.

I'm looking for someone who…

Appreciates art and doesn't have a fear of needles, for obvious reasons. Can I fill you in?

My perfect date has…

A completely bare back so that I can unleash my artistic desires upon it. I'll leave an indelible mark on both your skin and your heart.

HORI CHYO

The Smoking Hot Sámi

Josef Henriksen Buljo (1859–1925)

Occupation: Reindeer herder

Born: Kautokeino, Finnmark, Norway

Swipe if you like: A young Brad Pitt on ice, clad in reindeer furs

Danish-Norwegian photographer, Sophus Tromholt, captured this enthralling image of Sámi man Josef Henriksen Buljo during a trip to northern Norway between 1883–1884.

Trompholt, a teacher, astrophysicist and amateur photographer, went to this area of Norway to photograph the northern lights. While there, Trompholt became fascinated with the Sámi, the indigenous people of Norway, Sweden and Finland. At this time many Sámi's livelihood was reliant on reindeer herding, fishing and fur-trapping, so Buljo is more than likely to have worked in one or more of these trades. Buljo is shown as he was, beautifully unaffected: a dusting of melting snow in his hair, eyes narrowed in the glare of the bright sunlight, quietly smoking a pipe.

I'll fall for you if...

You look good in a Gákti and can outfish me under the midnight sun. Reindeer snacks are optional, but highly encouraged.

My best chat-up line is...

Are you a Northern light? Because you just brightened up my night sky. Your lavvu or mine?

The Teutonic Tenor

Albert Wolfe/De Cortez Wolffungen (1865–1931)

Occupation: Singing teacher, tenor and chorus director

Born: Hungen, Hesse, Germany

Swipe if you like: Spontaneous operatic outbursts in public

Who doesn't love a bit of an eccentric? Add good looks, talent and a flair for dressing and you've got yourself a man you'll treasure. A prime example is Herr Wolfe (who later changed his name to De Cortez Wolffungen). Born in Germany, Albert trained as a singer, moving to the US in 1900. As a singing teacher and director of opera choruses, Albert worked across the US, including at Philadelphia's Griffith Hall and the Twentieth Century Club in Buffalo, New York. He opened one show himself, singing an aria from *Der Freischütz* using the original German text. Wolffungen received praise in the local press for his 'voice of excellent range and quality and much to dramatic fervour'.

You'll win me over if…

You applaud wildly after my morning shower arias and tolerate my enlivened debates about the superiority of tenors.

Dating me is like…

Attending a German opera – dramatic, intense and sometimes over the top, but you'll be left with an unforgettable experience.

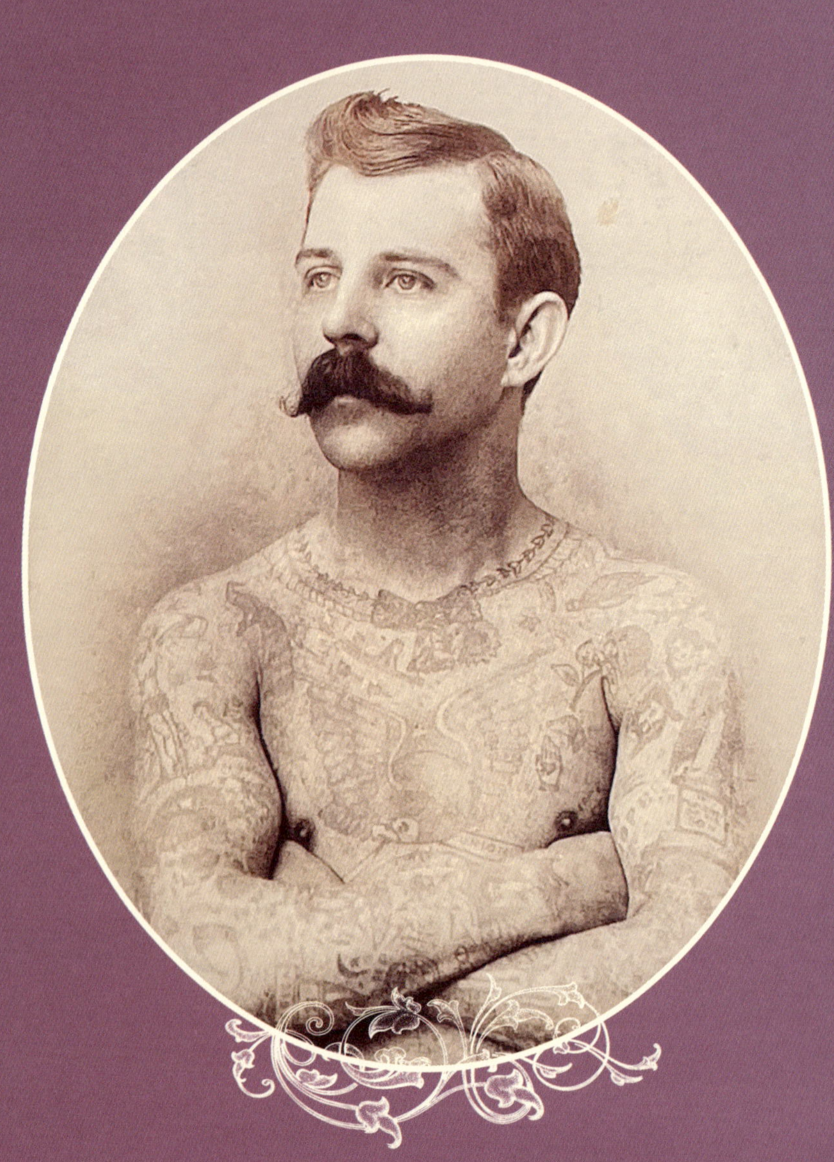

Only Skin Deep

Franklin Howard Packard AKA Professor Frank Howard (1857–1925)

Occupation: Tattoo artist and showman

Born: Providence, Rhode Island, US

Swipe if you like: Tattoos and 'taches

'Professor' Franklin Howard Packard was the 'Original Tattooed Man'. He first got inked when he was captured by Native Americans, about the age of 15, when he was a drummer boy with the Regiment to the Western Frontier at Fort Russell. While in captivity, Frank met another prisoner, with a flair for tattoos. Frank got a small tattoo done on his arm, later going back after his release to get a full body suit.

Word soon spread of this 'tattooed man', and Frank made an appearance at Brown University, allowing himself to be a lecture subject. It was here that he got the offer to appear at the Centennial Exhibition of 1876 in Philadelphia. This was the beginning of a long and successful career as a showman, with Frank being paid to showcase his tattoos at museums and circuses (namely, freak shows). Capitalizing on his fame, Frank opened a tattoo shop in Boston in 1902 and also sold mail-order tattoo machines and supplies.

I'm the kind of guy…

Who will strip off at the merest mention of 'tattoo'. I've got a lot to show and even more to tell.

Hot Victorians started as the Instagram account (@hotvictorians) in the summer of 2019. I came to the idea by thinking about all the times I'd seen photographs and paintings from the 1800s and early 1900s depicting a strikingly handsome man. I wondered if others had noticed and appreciated them as I did. I thought there must be an Instagram account that would cater to my admiration of males from times long past. The term 'hot Victorians' came instantly to mind, and I searched for an account along those lines, but none came up. So, I decided to wear the (top) hat, don the mantle of account curator, and create one myself. With the name, handle and hashtag all unified under 'hotvictorians', the rest is history (pun intended).

From the outset, I was keen to have an account that gave some historical information along with tantalizing imagery. I wanted the chance (wherever possible) to share snippets of the lives of the gentlemen I featured. With the world very much polarized in recent years, I wanted to showcase men of all races, religions, backgrounds and sexualities. If they were handsome and within the timeframe, I'd set myself (Victorian: 1837–1901, and Edwardian: 1901–10), they were a candidate for @hotvictorians. I originally had the end of the Edwardian era as the cutoff, but after coming across some unmissable images from later in the 1910s, I decided to use some aesthetic licence and extended it to 1919.

Aside from myself searching, collecting and selecting the chaps, I invited followers to contribute by nominating someone they had come across, be it a dashing ancestor or an attractive unknown man they found in a collection of cabinet cards in a junk shop. The followship grew and people understood what the angle and intentions of the account were. Between the history facts, and spotlighting of lesser-known people I felt needed attention, I also let my inner romance novelist run amok. Think mid-20th-century pulp fiction in Dickensian garb with a touch of Merchant Ivory drama and you're halfway there.

One of the most fascinating aspects of @hotvictorians has been the opportunity to challenge the rather stagnant view of the people of the 19th and early 20th centuries. They were not a monolith of repression and conformity but clearly had the strong human impulses that we have had since the dawn of time: to be noticed, admired and remembered.

By carefully choosing photographs and placing them in the context of modern social media, @hotvictorians underlines how self-presentation has always been an art form. The juxtaposition of Instagram's modernity with the old images, brings the sitters closer to us. In an age where digital self-expression is at an all-time high, *Hot Victorians* serves as a playful, yet poignant, reminder that the desire to curate one's image, to be seen, and to leave something of the self behind is anything but modern – it's timeless.

Aside from the chaps in the photographs themselves, none of this would have been possible without the wonderful followers of @hotvictorians. Your enthusiasm, playful comments and fantastic submissions have made this account what it is today. Every shared photograph, every intriguing factoid, and every suggestively appreciative remark adds to the joy of uncovering these long-gone but forever dashing gentlemen. Thank you for being part of this journey through time, for celebrating history with humour and heart. Here's to many more discoveries, discussions and deliciously dapper gents from the past.

Dedicated to the most important of gentlemen who have shaped my own history, Rudolph, Henry and Mic.

Born in London, a city renowned for its museums, Aaron Radford-Wattley is a lifelong history enthusiast. From dragging his parents around every castle in the UK since he could walk, to doing his senior school work experience at Christie's auctioneers, Aaron has always had a love for the past.

At nine years of age, Aaron bought his first 19th century photograph, an 1880s cabinet card, at a fair celebrating the centenary of the psychiatric hospital (a former Victorian asylum) where his father worked. Thus began a lifelong fascination with antique photographs which, to this day, he continues to collect. His other love, the English language and the written word, led him into a 20-year career specializing in copywriting, journalism and digital content editing.

Currently residing in New York, Aaron spends his free time researching his own genealogy, visiting museums, attending performances at the Lincoln Center, and visiting friends and family in the UK and Ireland whenever he can.

This book would not have been possible without Andrew Roff and his inspiring vision and endless encouragement.

Image Credits

3 Pepita Milmore Memorial Fund 4 Museum of Fine Arts of Cordoba/ Photographic collection of the Romero de Torres family 23 Topley Studio/ Library and Archives Canada 31 Freud Museum London 35 Somerset County Historical Society 38 Library of Congress Prints and Photographs Division 40 Library of Congress Prints and Photographs Division 43 The Joseph M. Cohen Family Collection 47 Bridgeman Images 51 Library of Congress/ The Bain Collection 52 Newark Memories 54 Library of Congress 57 Courtesy of Toronto Public Library 58 Getty Images 61 National Baseball Hall of Fame and Museum 62 Mary Evans Picture Library/Graham Hales Collection 65 Newark memories 66 Bob Thomas/Popperfoto/Getty Images 69 Agence Meurisse 73 Mary Evans Picture Library 75 The National Archives, ref. COPY1/392 81 Theodore Roosevelt Collection, Harvard College Library 85 Pepita Milmore Memorial Fund 86 Amon Carter Museum of American Art 88 Paul Stokey 91 Nebraska State Historical Society 92 Collection of the Smithsonian National Museum of African American History and Culture 99 Amon Carter Museum of American Art 104 Library of Congress Prints and Photographs Division 112 Wellcome Collection 114 Getty Images 117 New York Public Library 121 Houghton Library, Harvard University 122 Library of Congress 125 Wellcome Collection 126 The Burns Archive 129 Library of Congress Prints and Photographs Division Washington, D.C. 130 Wellcome Collection 133 Collection of the Smithsonian National Museum of African American History and Culture 134 public domain 136 The New York Public Library/The Miriam and Ira D. Wallach Division of Art, Prints and Photographs 138 PhotoMuse Collection/Herbert Ascherman Collection 141 Bridgeman Images 142 Museum of Fine Arts of Cordoba/Photographic collection of the Romero de Torres family 146 Collection of the Smithsonian National Museum of African American History and Culture 149 Bridgeman Images 150 The New York Public Library/ The Miriam and Ira D. Wallach Division of Art, Prints and Photographs 154 Getty Museum Collection 157 Photo Library of the Civic Museums of History and Art 158 Unknown Photographer. Rupert Bunny in Provence c.1884 161 Getty Museum Collection 162 Courtesy L. Tom Perry Special Collections, Harold B. Lee Library, Brigham Young University 165 Nagasaki University Library 166 Sophus Tromholt/The Picture Collection at the University of Bergen Library 169 Submitted by Charles Almon 170 Collection of Nick Vaccaro

Cover image Paul Stokey

First published in Great Britain in 2025 by

Greenfinch
An imprint of Quercus Editions Ltd
Carmelite House
50 Victoria Embankment
London EC4Y 0DZ

An Hachette UK company
The representative in the EEA is Hachette Ireland, 8 Castlecourt Centre, Dublin 15, D15 XTP3, Ireland (email: info@hbgi.ie)

A CIP catalogue record for this book is available from the British Library

HB ISBN 978-1-52944-665-4
Ebook ISBN 978-1-52944-666-1

10 9 8 7 6 5 4 3

Design by Mietta Yans
Project management by Becky Alexander

Printed and bound in China by C&C Offset Printing Co., Ltd.

Papers used by Greenfinch are from well-managed forests and other responsible sources